10/10

DATE DUE

the
make today matter
makeover

the
make today matter
makeover

THE 26 BEST WAYS TO
Recapture Daily Magic,
Kick-start High-Energy Living,
and Get the Most out of Life

Brook Noel

 SOURCEBOOKS, INC.®
NAPERVILLE, ILLINOIS

Published by Sourcebooks, Inc.
P.O. Box 4410, Naperville, Illinois 60567-4410
(630) 961-3900
Fax: (630) 961-2168
www.sourcebooks.com

Library of Congress Cataloging-in-Publication Data

Noel, Brook.
  The make today matter makeover : the 26 best ways to recapture daily magic, kick-start high-energy living, and get the most out of life / by Brook Noel.
      p. cm.
  1. Self-actualization (Psychology) 2. Change (Psychology) 3. Self-help techniques. 4. Happiness. I. Title.
  BF637.S4N64 2009
  646.7--dc22

2009030719

Printed and bound in the United States of America.
DR 10 9 8 7 6 5 4 3 2 1

For Sammy…
Thank you for making every day matter.

contents

acknowledgments

I am honored and privileged to have so many individuals who have contributed to the creation of this book. First and foremost I would like to thank the Make Today Matter Community members for their feedback, enthusiasm, and words of wisdom. A special thanks to my right hand and MTM director Rhonda Miga—said simply, you rock! Lyn Witter, thank you for your continued work in bringing forth the spirit of community through your contribution as community coordinator. I would also like to thank the more than thirty-five volunteers who help hundreds of women make each day matter.

I would also like to thank Dan Miga for his support and for letting me borrow Rhonda so often! And of course, my husband Andy—I am so excited that you have recently joined me in my work, and I look forward to many shared years of helping others. My daughter Sammy, I thank you from the bottom of my heart for your support, help, and laughter. As far as assistants go you are the best in the world.

To my mom—thank you for your years of friendship, support, brainstorming, and M&M talks. I cherish our relationship more than you know, and I am lucky to have such an intelligent, creative mother and role model. I love you.

A big shout of thanks to my editor, Sara Appino. If there was an Oscar awarded for patience, I am sure you would win. Thank you for your belief and support, and a big thanks to all the rest of the Sourcebooks crew who continue to guide and support my books and writing career. A special thank you to the sales team at Sourcebooks, whose enthusiasm and energy is unparalleled. Additionally, I would like to thank a few people heavily involved in *The Make Today Matter Makeover*: Regan Fisher, Dawn Pope, Will Riley, Tina Silva, Ashley Haag, Danielle Trejo, Erika Koff, Barbara Hague, and Amy LaBudde. I am fortunate to have this awesome crew and independent publisher as my home.

Last, but never least, I thank God for giving me the path that He has and the guidance to take the steps I have taken and make the choices I have made. Life is rarely easy, but His light has always shown the way, and I will always follow.

Visit www.maketodaymatter.net and click on Freebies to download full-size copies of the worksheets used in this book.

"Nothing is worth more than this day." — *Goethe*

PART ONE

creating your make today matter road map

the make today matter journey

"Every morning you are handed 24 golden hours. They are one of the few things in this world that you get free of charge. If you had all the money in the world, you couldn't buy an extra hour. What will you do with this priceless treasure?" —*Anonymous*

It has been said that life is what happens while we are making other plans. If today you stopped and took inventory of your life-to-date, how has your life path differed from the path you planned? Have life events and circumstances caused unexpected twists and turns? Perhaps a divorce, chance meeting, step-family, illness, job change, promotion, or loss have catapulted you in a direction you never foresaw when planning the future.

When I was in elementary school, I remember my father telling me he was moving to the Virgin Islands. Although I did not know where the Virgin Islands were, I guessed they were nowhere close to my then-Wisconsin home. While my parents had divorced when I was eight months old, my father and I had reestablished a relationship that was about to be severed just as it had been years before. As a young child I gained an introduction into how little control we often have over events that may largely influence our life path.

This would not be the only unexpected turn. In my teens I would leave high school two years early and uncover a talent, passion, and love for writing. My twenties would bring the tragic and sudden death of my only sibling, marriage, the birth of my daughter, an unexpected move across country, and nurturing a new and volatile business. The trend continued into my thirties (I am thirty-five at the time of this writing) with another cross country move, my husband's unexpected job loss, the tragic loss of my father, the sale of one business, and the exciting start of a new one.

Interestingly, despite the ups and downs I have always remained an obvious optimist. More than once I have been asked "How do you keep such a good attitude?" Only recently have I been able to put my optimism into words. I realize that over the years I have learned to stop looking at the path I had wanted to take and instead look at the path life has given me. I find magic where I am instead of dreaming about the magic I might have missed. I no longer spend countless hours planning how my life will unfold. Instead, I spend that time living the days I have. I have quit worrying about big milestones and instead focus on making each day matter.

Will Rogers once offered this simple and wise advice, "Never let yesterday use up too much of today." While we will all have days, weeks, months, or even years we would like to change, we cannot change them. If we spend today looking backward, what type of tomorrow will we create?

> *My formula for living optimistically is quite simple: Stop asking "Why me?" and begin asking "Now what?"*

The culmination of my life experiences led me to create the Make Today Matter Life System (MTM) in 2008. A comprehensive, online support and learning community, each day hundreds of members utilize MTM to stay focused on what we can control and letting go of what we cannot. We balance a little planning with a lot of action to create successful days that in turn create successful weeks, months, and years.

In the MTM System, after working through an online 30 Step Toolbox that covers time management, organization, clutter control, energy, routines, and attitude we take a monthly Snapshot and then choose three Minis to help support the areas where we want to grow and improve. We look at little, effective, realistic steps. This book brings the Snapshot and twenty-six MTM member-selected Minis to you in a do-it-yourself format.

The Minis cover a wide terrain. Use the first chapters of this book to help you work through the Snapshot, identify your priorities, and chart your unique path through this book. By doing so you will uncover what life areas are out of alignment and find proven strategies for effective change. The Mini-Makeovers provide short, achievable steps that fit into today's busy lifestyles. You do not need extensive planning or time. All you need is a commitment to letting go of what you cannot control and a mind-set ready to focus on what action you can take today to steer your life—to make the most of these twenty-four hours—to make today matter. Perhaps Maria Edgeworth said it best when she said, "If we take care of the moments, the years will take care of themselves." Now is your moment to begin. When you are ready, meet me at Chapter Two and we'll get moving.

CHAPTER TWO

your personal snapshot

"The definition of insanity is doing the same thing over and over and expecting different results."—*Albert Einstein*

Often we buy a book, program, workbook, or audiotape because the topic or "promise" strikes a chord. On a whim, we make the purchase, hoping it will help us create change. Usually it doesn't. When we approach change without clearly assessing our needs, our needs will be impossible to fulfill. <u>We cannot find a solution without first identifying what needs solving</u>.

We will begin this journey by taking a Snapshot of your life. The Snapshot Tool allows us to assess your life objectively and create a map that works through this book in the way it will best help you.

Snapshot Basics and Preparation

In *The Change Your Life Challenge* we use a Snapshot covering seventeen Life Areas. For this journey, we will be using an abbreviated Snapshot covering six of the areas that women ask me for help with most often:

- Time & Information Management
- Household Management & Maintenance
- Goals & Career
- Self-Time & Self-Discovery
- Energy & Health
- Attitude & Self-Esteem

Next to each Life Area is a row of boxes numbered one through ten. A ten represents high-priority areas during this season of your life, whereas a one represents an area of lower importance. I use the term "seasons of life" because priorities often shift. Sometimes these shifts occur monthly, other times quarterly, other times annually or every couple of years.

This Snapshot is not meant to capture your priorities for your entire life — only the current season and your priorities today, at this moment. The reasoning is simple: We cannot change tomorrow; we cannot change yesterday. The only place we have the power to create change is here and now.

If you do not want to write in your book, before reading further make a photocopy or print an additional copy of the Snapshot by visiting www. maketodaymatter.net and clicking the Freebies link.

Step One: Defining Your Journey Numbers

Begin by carefully considering the category in the first row, time management. How important is time management to you right now? If it is very important, circle one of the higher numbers. If it is not important to you right now, choose one of the lower numbers. If it is somewhere between high importance and low importance, choose one of the middle numbers. The circled number reflects how important this area is to you *right now*. It does not reflect where you currently perceive yourself to be, where you think you should be, or where you are in comparison to your next-door neighbor.

As women, we often fall into the "please everyone — sacrifice ourselves" trap. We want to be everything to everyone and then ride the roller coaster of guilt when we cannot achieve this impossible standard. I know what that Snapshot looks like — I've tried it. I do not want to see that on your worksheet. Instead, I want you to try something that might be a bit foreign: let your choices be reflective of what *you* truly want from *your* life, not what others want for you or what will make others happy.

When our life is out of balance, every Life Area may be clamoring for our attention. We may feel the urge to give every category an eight, nine, or ten. Limit yourself to one nine and one ten. We have to prioritize to take effective action, and to prioritize, we need to choose and weigh each area carefully. A lower number <u>does not mean</u> the area is not important or will be ignored; a lower number only indicates that other Life Areas are higher on your life radar *at the moment*.

Keep in mind that no one will see this Snapshot. It is just for you. The only "right answer" is honesty. Our Snapshot is as unique as our thumbprint. Maybe your high-importance areas would seem odd to another person. We aren't creating this Snapshot for another person. We are creating this Snapshot to help you identify and create a path to fulfill the unique needs that brought you to this book.

Work through each of the six Snapshot categories in the same way.

Please complete this step before continuing.

Abbreviated Snapshot Worksheet

Life Area	Current Priority										Journey Number (circled)	Life Number (Squared)	Tally
Time & Information Management	1	2	3	4	5	6	7	8	9	10			
Energy & Health	1	2	3	4	5	6	7	8	9	10			
Home Management & Maintenance	1	2	3	4	5	6	7	8	9	10			
Self-Time & Self-Discovery	1	2	3	4	5	6	7	8	9	10			
Attitude & Self-Esteem	1	2	3	4	5	6	7	8	9	10			
Goals & Career	1	2	3	4	5	6	7	8	9	10			

Step Two: You Are Here!

Uncovering Your Life Numbers

The completed area of the Snapshot indicates how <u>you would like your life to look</u>. Your next step is to identify where you are *right now* in relation to your Journey Numbers.

Look at your number in the time management category. How would that number "look" in your life? What would change? Take a moment to imagine how your life would be different at the number you marked in Step One.

Next consider how well you currently manage time. Which of the following statements best describes the relationship between your day-to-day reality and your number from Step One?

- My Step One number and my current reality are the same.
- My current reality needs to change in order to reach my Step One number.
- My current reality exceeds my Step One number.

Now place a square around a number that reflects your answer. (We use a square so we can keep the two numbers separate.) For example:

- If your Step One number and current reality are the same, place a square around your Step One number.
- If your current reality needs to change in order to reach your Step One number, place a square around a number below your Step One number. The larger the gap between your current reality and your ideal, the lower you would place the square.
- If your current reality exceeds your ideal, place a square around a number above the number circled in Step One. The more you exceed your ideal, the higher you would place the square.

The numbers you mark with squares are called your Life Numbers. Work through each category and mark a Life Number.

Please complete this step before continuing.

Step Three: Summarizing Your Findings

We now have two types of information about your life:

- **Journey Profile:** The Journey Profile is composed of all the circled Journey Numbers in Step One and provides an overview of where you want to get to on your journey.
- **Life Profile:** The Life Profile is comprised of all of the squared Life Numbers and provides an overview of where you are today in your life.

Our last step involves merging these two findings together to create an Action Snapshot.

The right-most column is labeled "tally." Subtract your squared number from the circled number and write the result in this box.

For example, if you circled a nine in finances for your Journey Number in Step One and then placed a square around five for your Life Number in Step Two, the total would be four (9 – 5 = 4). If your Journey Number was a six and your Life Number eight, the tally would be negative two (6 – 8 = –2). These numbers form the foundation for the Action Plan we will create in the next chapter.

CHAPTER THREE

charting your course

"You can have it all...just not at the same time."—*Unknown*

Educational systems have reasons they limit the number of majors students can take in a four-year-college program: time, focus, and success rank high among them. Imagine if one hundred students decided to declare five majors simultaneously, and in four years, they aimed to complete marine biology, art history, mass communications, psychiatry, and primary education. Given the time and focus required by each major, what do you think the success rate of these one hundred students would be?

No matter what the students' willpower, intelligence, desire, optimism, stamina, or energy level, this lofty goal could not be reached. There are not enough hours in a day to complete five demanding majors in a four-year period.

In the end, all of these students would fail. Does this mean they are bad students? Of course not (although they may interpret incompletion as failure). The missing link is not in their attitude, energy, or ability to take action. The missing component is time.

Change requires focus, and focus requires time. In order to achieve change, we need to replace ingrained habits with new actions and choices. Trying to implement multiple lofty changes in addition to maintaining day-to-day responsibilities creates an environment not conducive to focus. Without focus, we cannot complete what we start.

Focus, not desire or willpower, is at the core of cycling through one program after another. Without a clearly defined plan for change containing concise action steps, we are swimming upstream. This book, along with *The Change Your Life Challenge* and my online program, are designed to encourage focus, which in turn increases the success rate of lasting lifestyle change.

Completing the Action Plan

It is time to chart your course through this book, using the information we gathered in the last chapter.

Find the Action Plan worksheet, take the tallies from your Snapshot (Journey Number minus Life Number), and then follow these steps:

1. **Zero:**
   Look for any categories that equal zero. A zero means that your results and priority are in alignment. Write the names of these categories in the Balanced: Manage & Maintain section. (Don't worry if you don't have any zeroes — you will soon!)

2. **Negative Numbers:**
   Look for any negative numbers in your Snapshot tally column. (Don't worry if you don't have any negative numbers — few women do at the start.) A negative number means you are more than satisfied with your results in relation to the priority of that category in your life. If any of your negatively numbered categories involve a lot of time, consider scaling back your time to better align with the result you seek. Time gained can be used to focus on areas that are out of alignment. Write the names of any negative categories in either the Scale Back or Balanced: Manage & Maintain section.

3. **Positive Numbers:**
   Transfer the remaining categories and their tally numbers to the Action Plan worksheet. These are the Life Areas that need your attention. List these numbers from high to low in the Life Areas Needing Attention section.

Please complete this step before continuing.

Action Plan Worksheet

Date Completed: _____

Balanced: Manage & Maintain

_____

_____

_____

Scale Back:

_____

_____

_____

Life Areas Needing Attention (list from high to low):

_____

_____

_____

Notes:

_____

_____

_____

Reading the Results

We become stressed, overwhelmed, tired, and emotionally drained when our actions do not align with our values. Your Journey Numbers offer a glimpse of how strongly you value each category at this phase of your life. Your Life Numbers reveal how closely your actions match your values. Your Action Snapshot total provides a glimpse at which Life Areas have the largest gap between your actions and values; the higher the number, the greater the gap. Closing these gaps is the pathway to contentment.

The list you created in the Action Plan worksheet is the foundation for a road map to work through this book. By shrinking the biggest gaps first, we recover energy, emotional well-being, and focus while creating forward momentum throughout the program.

The Make Today Matter Road Map worksheet lists all of the Mini-Makeovers in this book. I recommend choosing one or two Mini-Makeovers to work on each month and finishing one before moving on to the next. Using your Action Plan as a guide, find the Minis that match the Life Areas Needing Attention on your Action Plan. Prioritize these in the order you will complete them.

Please complete this step before continuing.

Tip: Choosing a Mini is only the first step; completing the Mini is most important. In each Mini you will find an Action Step Checklist. Use these quick reference checklists to help you break down the Mini, and schedule time into your calendar to work it through to completion.

Make Today Matter Road Map Worksheet

- **Energy & Health**
  ____ Refueling: Creating an Energy Map
  ____ Keeping a Food Diary
  ____ The Caffeine Culprit
  ____ Nine Steps to Breaking a Bad Habit

- **Household Management & Maintenance**
  ____ Simplifying Your Wardrobe
  ____ Creating a Recipe Library
  ____ Mastering Meal Planning
  ____ Controlling Your Cosmetics
  ____ Beautifying Your Home
  ____ Responsibilities and Rewards

- **Goals & Career**
  ____ Creating a Goal Grab Bag
  ____ Mind Mapping
  ____ Effective Project Management
  ____ Seven-Day Anti-Stress Regimen

- **Time & Information Management**
  ____ The Ten Faces of Procrastination
  ____ Overcoming Magazine Madness: Creating a Personal Reference Library
  ____ Little Time Blocks
  ____ Reality Routines

- **Self-Time & Self-Discovery**
  ____ Creating a Goal and Treasure Book
  ____ Journaling toward Self-Discovery
  ____ Journaling for Answers: Digging Deeper
  ____ The Movie in Your Mind

- **Attitude & Self-Esteem**
  ____ Staying Centered
  ____ Recapturing Daily Magic Part One: Back to Basics
  ____ Recapturing Daily Magic Part Two: Beyond Ourselves
  ____ Facing Fear and Stepping outside the Comfort Zone

PART TWO

the mini-makeovers

energy & health

Tired? Emotionally drained? Wishing you could put the skip back into your step and greet each day with renewed passion and purpose? The Mini-Makeovers in this section will help you uncover energy drainers and restore and renew your energy level.

Mini-Makeovers
- Refueling: Creating an Energy Map
- Keeping a Food Diary
- The Caffeine Culprit
- Nine Steps to Breaking a Bad Habit

mini-makeover

refueling: creating an energy map

"Energy and persistence alter all things."—*Benjamin Franklin*

As kids we had too much energy, and as adults we can't seem to find a formula to reclaim it. What happened? Where did this energy-loss epidemic come from? And more importantly, what can we do about it?

Action Step Checklist

- ☐ Read the Creating Your Energy Log section and print or photocopy your logs.
- ☐ Mark the first log with today's date and record what you can for the day thus far.
- ☐ Complete seven logs before proceeding to the Energy Mapping section.
- ☐ Complete your first Energy Map.
- ☐ Create your first Trend Analysis and attach it to your map.
- ☐ Continue creating your Energy Maps until you can clearly see the strongest energy-influencing factors in your life.

In my research and experience I have spent countless hours studying the elusive concept of energy. For many, energy is like happiness: you keep chasing it, and just when you think you have it cornered, it sneaks out a window and the search begins again. I have watched people change sleeping, eating, and physical activity patterns (often in extreme ways), only to end up more exhausted than when they began.

I began to approach "energy" as a math problem. Certainly two plus two wasn't always adding up to four. People who slept the recommended hours per night and followed rigid health guidelines were still tired. For many, regardless of how they approached two plus two, it equaled zero fuel. What became apparent was that many variables must be involved—and even those variables likely had variables of their own, and all of those variables likely varied from person to person.

I attentively researched, applied, and studied these variables at work in people's lives. This research wasn't conducted in any formal lab, because we do not live in formal labs. It was done in real life while facing real challenges.

What I can conclude with confidence is that our unique energy formula is as unique as our thumbprint. Each of us is influenced by different factors in different ways. Some of us might be more emotionally resilient than others, while others find emotional challenges zap our energy stores. Some of us might be influenced more by sugar, food dye, or carbs than others. The only way to discover your unique energy pattern is to become a detective in your own life and watch how the many energy variables influence the way you live.

This Mini is divided into three sections:

1. Keeping a daily Energy Log
2. Mapping daily logs into one-week graphs
3. Analyzing your findings and making changes

ENERGY LOG
Sleep and Rest

	Energy Level: 0 = ready to sleep 10 = great energy	Mood: 0 = pessimistic 10 = optimistic	Quality of Last Night's Sleep: 0 = poor sleep 10 = good sleep
Wake time: _____			
Bed time: _____			
Nap time *(if you rested — eyes closed — please list what time you lay down and what time you stood up):* _____ to _____	Energy before nap _____ Energy after nap _____	Mood before nap _____ Mood after nap _____	
Total hours slept in 24-hour period:			

Caffeine and Water Consumption

Type of caffeine consumed and amount (coffee, tea, soda; 6 ounces, 12 ounces, etc.)		List any plain water you consumed (not water found in Crystal Light, etc.) and amount	
Type / Amount / Time	Type / Amount / Time	Amount / Time Consumed	Amount / Time Consumed

Food Consumption

Meal	Time Consumed	General Description of Meal/Snack
Breakfast:		
Lunch:		
Dinner:		
Other:		

Activities
Exercise: Activity: _____ Minutes: _____

Did you do anything just for you today, such as a hobby, reading, etc.?

Self-Care: Activity: _____ Minutes: _____

Stress & Attitude

Scale for all questions except #2:
1 = very negative   2 = negative   3 = neutral 4 = positive 5 = very positive

Scale for question #2:
1 = very stressed 2 = pretty stressed 3 = average 4 = low stress 5 = zero to little stress

   As you complete these steps consistently, you will see patterns and trends begin to emerge that reveal how you can maximize and restore your energy.

Interactions with Others					
1. How would you rate the affect on your energy from your interaction with adults today?					
2. How would you rate the stress encountered from interaction with adults today?					
Attitude and Thought Patterns					
3. How would you rate your overall thoughts throughout the day?					
4. What rating would you give to your morning overall?					
5. What rating would you give to your afternoon overall?					
6. What rating would you give to your evening overall?					

Step One: Creating an Energy Log

Photocopy seven copies of the Energy Log, or visit www. maketodaymatter.net to download a free full-size worksheet. Store your logs somewhere they can travel with you throughout the day. If you use a Catch-All Notebook, that is the perfect spot. Otherwise a planner, calendar—anything that stays with you most of the day—will work.

Mark the first log with today's date and record what you can for the day thus far. The instructions for completing the Energy Log are printed directly on the log sheet. For the next seven days, complete a new log each day. Once you have seven, proceed to Step Two.

Please complete this step before continuing.

Complete if applicable:

If you are currently diagnosed with a physical illness (chronic fatigue, cancer, fibromyalgia, arthritis), please rate how much this condition negatively influenced your physical and emotional health today (one being the lowest; ten being the highest)._____

If you are currently being treated for depression, ADD, anxiety, or other mood disorder, please rate how much this condition negatively influenced your physical and emotional health today (one being the lowest; ten being the highest)._____

Notes:

_____

_____

_____

_____

_____

_____

_____

_____

Step Two: How to Map Your Progress

We need a clear way to measure what works and what does not in our lives. Math is the best measurement: we can watch, study, and compare our patterns, identifying which factors create the most productive days. Over time, this reveals the pattern that optimizes our functionality.

The Weekly Energy Mapping worksheet will help you identify these trends. Don't worry; the math is easy, and looking at the results is often revealing and fun. Once a week, transfer your daily Energy Logs to the Weekly Energy Mapping worksheet. Keep in mind you do not have to do this forever—just until you begin seeing correlations in your energy patterns.

Weekly Mapping Worksheet

www.maketodaymatter.net

Analysis for week of _____

Weely sleep source

	1 Energy	2 Mood	3 Sleep Quality	4 Water (Percentage of Goal)	5 Morning RaRating	6 Afternoon Rating	7 Evening Rating	8 Interaction	9 Caffeine	10 Stress	11 Total*	12 Bed Time	13 Wake Time	14 Total Night Sleep	15 Nap (if any)	16 Total Sleep 24 hour Period	17 Breakfast	18 Vitamin
Monday	10	10	10	10=100%	5	5	5	5	10=100	5	MON						YES NO	YES NO
Tuesday	9	9	9	9=90%	4	4	4	4	9=200	4	TUE						YES NO	YES NO
Wednesday	8	8	8	8=80%	3	3	3	3	8=300	3	WED						YES NO	YES NO
Thursday	7	7	7	7=70%	2	2	2	2	7=400	2	THU						YES NO	YES NO
Friday	6	6	6	6=60%	1	1	1	1	6=500	1	FRI						YES NO	YES NO
Saturday	5	5	5	5=50%					5=600		SAT						YES NO	YES NO
Sunday	4	4	4	4=40%					4=700		SUN						YES NO	YES NO
	3	3	3	3=30%					3=800		TOTAL							
	2	2	2	2=20%					2=900									
	1	1	1	1=10% or less					1=1000 or more									

Weely sleep source

*Instructions for column 11: Total the number in columns 1 through 10 each day. Once you have completed columns 1 through 10, total them and write the sum for each day on the bottom or backside of the worksheet.

Consult the Weekly Energy Mapping worksheet on the next page, and refer to it as you read through these instructions. Complete each step before moving on to the next.

How to Use the Weekly Energy Mapping Worksheet

The first time you complete this worksheet, it will take longer to learn the columns and how it works. Once you have done this once or twice, it should only take a few moments to complete.

Begin by filling in the dates of the week you are analyzing at the top of the worksheet.

Tip: I have found that it is easiest to plot and analyze your results by using a different color for each day of the week. If you choose to use a red marker, pencil, or crayon for Monday, place a little red dot near the word "Monday" so you can easily remember what the red line you will be creating represents.

In the black row at the top, the columns are numbered one through eighteen. The very first column contains the seven days of the week.

- **Instructions for columns one through eight:** These numbers are transferred directly from your Energy Log. Begin with your first colored marker (let's say you are using red for Monday), and put a small dot on the number that represents what you recorded in your log. For example, if my mood from my Energy Log was an eight, I would put a red dot on or near the eight. Continue doing this for columns one through seven. Fill in all of Monday with your first color (in my example that would be red). Then connect the dots with the red pen, which will give you a line that looks somewhat like a stock-market graph.

  Once you are done with Monday, choose another color and repeat the process for Tuesday; then choose another color and repeat the process for Wednesday, etc.

- **Instructions for column nine:** The numbers in this column represent milligrams of caffeine consumed and range from

100 to 1,000. Place a dot by the number closest to your caffeine consumption. If you consume 1,000 milligrams or more, mark the 1,000 box. If you do not consume any caffeine, mark the top of the 100 box. Note: You will see that these selections are labeled 10 = 100, 9 = 200, etc. The second number is the milligrams (100 or 200 milligrams). The first number is the number you use when adding up the columns as instructed in column eleven.

To determine how much caffeine is in a beverage, please visit this website: mayoclinic.com/health/caffeine/AN01211.

Tip: *The Caffeine Culprit Mini-Makeover in this section covers caffeine in detail.*

- **Instructions for column ten:** Column ten is somewhat subjective and is based on the amount of stress you felt that specific day. Think of one as a very stressful day and five as an unstressful day.

  Make sure all of the dots in columns one through ten are now connected for each day of the week.

- **Instructions for column eleven:** Follow your "Monday line," and add all the numbers together (making sure to add the first number for the caffeine column, not the milligrams number) to arrive at a daily total. A higher total indicates positive changes and an energetic environment. The maximum score is seventy.

- **Reference columns twelve through eighteen:** All of these columns are basically self-explanatory. While you likely have this information in your journal or Energy Log, transferring it to this weekly summary is very helpful for analyzing patterns and effectiveness. We do not create a graph line like we did with the earlier columns. Instead, we record the information here for quick reference in the upcoming analysis.

- **Columns twelve and thirteen:** Simply record the time you went to bed and the time you awoke.
- **Column fourteen:** Write down the total hours of sleep you had for the night.
- **Column fifteen:** If you took a nap, write down the length in hours or minutes.
- **Column sixteen:** Add columns fourteen and fifteen together to arrive at your total sleep time.
- **Column seventeen:** Circle "yes" or "no" to indicate whether you ate breakfast.
- **Column eighteen:** Circle "yes" or "no" to indicate whether you took a multivitamin supplement.

Lastly, at the bottom of column eleven you will see a "total" box. Once you have an entire week mapped, total all of the numbers in column eleven and place the total in the box. This number allows us to easily compare one week to another in terms of total energy.

Step Three: Drawing Conclusions and Analyzing Trends

Once you have completed your Weekly Energy Mapping worksheet, begin looking for trends using the following questions as a springboard. For the best results, write or type your answers on a separate piece of paper and staple them to your worksheet.

- Which two days did you have the highest score in column eleven?
- Looking at the "graph line" created in columns one through ten, do you notice a pattern between the two days from the previous question?
- Regarding the reference notes in the remaining columns, do you detect any patterns among the good days?
- Which two days did you have the lowest score in column eleven?
- With the graph line created in columns one through ten, do you notice a pattern between these lower-energy days?

- Looking at the reference notes in the remaining columns, do you detect any patterns among the lowest days?
- On both the highest and lowest days, do you see any correlation between the day <u>preceding</u> the high or low day? For example, if you wake up with low energy on Tuesday, is there anything from Monday that could be a cause (lack of sleep, skipping breakfast, not enough water, etc.)?

Looking at all seven days, what correlation can you see between
- sleep and mood?
- sleep and energy?
- water and energy?
- mood and energy?
- sleep quality and sleep time?
- sleep quality and mood?
- stress and mood?
- stress and sleep quality?
- mood and interaction?
- caffeine and sleep quality?
- energy and nap?
- energy and total sleep?
- mood and total sleep?
- energy and interaction?

Is there a significant difference in your daily answer for columns five, six, and seven (morning rating, afternoon rating, evening rating)?

How are your answers in columns five, six, and seven influenced by
- nap?
- total sleep?
- breakfast?
- water?
- caffeine?

Which time is the most difficult for you energy-wise in columns five, six, and seven (morning rating, afternoon rating, evening rating)? What energy ideas could help you during this time (drinking a glass of ice-cold water, a twenty-minute power nap, some deep-breathing exercises, etc.)?

For the first week or two, analyze each of the areas in Step Three. As you become more familiar with your patterns, you may not need to analyze each area. Instead, you can analyze the areas that are inconsistent or need the most improvement.

Finding Your Groove

As you collect multiple Energy Logs and Weekly Maps, begin looking at the <u>total</u> scores from column eleven to identify which weeks score higher. Then look for what is happening in the better- or higher-scoring weeks that is not happening in the lower-scoring ones. Continue working with these tools until you find that your energy is consistent and at a level that allows you to achieve your daily priorities.

mini-makeover

keeping a food diary

"Don't dig your grave with your own knife and fork."—*English proverb*

What if picking up a pen could more than double your weight-loss results? Would you be interested? Recent research conducted by Kaiser Permanente Center for Health Research (KPCHR) showed those who kept a food diary ended up losing twice as much weight as those who did not. This Mini will take you step by step through building and effectively using a food diary.

Action Step Checklist
- ☐ Record everything you eat for at least one week.
- ☐ Analyze your intake using the guidelines in this Mini.
- ☐ Complete a month analysis worksheet.
- ☐ Choose three simple changes based on your observations.

Writing down the "vitals" of your eating habits can help you uncover trends in your eating patterns and brainstorm healthier choices. "The more food records people kept, the more weight they lost," says Jack Hollis, PhD, a researcher at KPCHR and lead author of a study published in the *American Journal of Preventive Medicine.* "Those who kept daily food records lost twice as much weight as those who kept no records. It seems that the simple act of writing down what you eat encourages people to consume fewer calories."

This Mini is divided into two sections. First we will create and keep a Food Diary for seven days. You can use the pages provided in the book or print a full-size page free at www.maketodaymatter.net.

While you will want to maintain the food diary practice for long-term benefit, we need at least one week of entries to work through the second portion of this Mini, which focuses on healthy changes. Use the following guidelines to collect your first week of Food Diary entries.

Step One: Food Diary Basics

- **Write it down when you eat it.** Make sure to keep your Food Diary worksheet with you at all times. Get in the habit of writing down what you eat right after you eat it. If you wait until the end of the day, it can be hard to remember, or you may inadvertently overlook some items.
- **Make sure to include the amount.** Use whatever measure you can, such as "handful" or "two-by-two-inch piece."
- **Don't just record food—record mood.** On the Food Diary worksheet, you will see a place to record your mood. Moods dramatically affect our food consumption and will be an important part of the food-trend analysis we complete in the second portion of this Mini.
- **Report who, what, when, and where.** The Food Diary worksheet has a space to record who you were with and what you were doing when you ate. This information will help you analyze your specific food patterns and create healthy alternative strategies in the second part of this Mini.

- **Write everything down.** Keep your worksheet with you all day, and write down everything you eat or drink. This includes a piece of candy, a handful of chips, soda—everything. Don't forget to record condiments, too!

Tip: Do not be discouraged as you write down what you eat. Sometimes we may not like what we see! Do not use that realization as a reason to abandon the practice or skip the second part of the Mini or wait for a week where you "do better." It is not realistic to think you can change patterns overnight. The realizations you gain in part two will make any food diary the perfect step to begin making healthy changes in your life.

Once you have seven days recorded, move on to Step Two.

Please complete this step before continuing.

Step Two: Analyzing Your Food Diary

You may have already noticed that the process of writing down your food choices—at the same time you eat—has begun influencing your choices. Awareness is a key tool in this journey, since we often eat out of routine, boredom, or habit.

We may also eat because of our mood, being alone, or being with others. All of these variables you tracked in the Food Diary can help you see the trends in your healthy and unhealthy choices.

Food Diary Worksheet

Food or Drink

Time	Amount (Specifically)	Consumed	Location	Were you alone or with someone? Who?	What activity were you involved in?	What was your mood?

We are going to do an in-depth analysis of your Food Diary this first week. I believe this technique is very important as you establish a regular Food Diary routine—at least for the first month, as it will help you clearly see trends and patterns. Use the trend-analysis technique you learn in this Mini until you feel you understand—and have control over—your food choices.

Analyzing Your Intake

Refer to the Food Diary Analysis worksheet in this section as you read through these instructions.

At the top of the worksheet, you will see the columns are numbered one through thirty-one. These numbers correspond with the dates of the month. On the left-hand side are the hours of the day—spanning from 5:00 a.m. to 9:00 p.m.

- **Step One:** Using your Food Diary as your guide, locate the date in the top column. Find the first entry in the time options. Where the column and row intersect, make an <u>empty</u> circle with red, blue, or black ink as follows:

  - Use a red circle to denote an unhealthy choice.
  - Use a black circle to denote a choice that is "so-so."
  - Use a blue circle to denote a healthy choice.

The following example shows a person who made a so-so choice on the fifth of the month in the 6:00 a.m. hour.

Month of:																															
Time *Date →*	1	2	3	4	5	6	7	8	9	10	11	12	13	14	15	16	17	18	19	20	21	22	23	24	25	26	27	28	29	30	31
4:00 AM																															
5:00 AM																															
6:00 AM				O																											
7:00 AM																															
8:00 AM																															

Continue working through the day in this fashion until you have put in a circle for each entry on your Food Diary.

A note for snackers: If you tend to have both snacks and meals, you may want to list them separately. Use circles to represent meals and squares to represent snacks, high-caloric coffees, and other non-meal food choices. Use the exact same color-coding system (red, blue, or black).

- **Step Two:** Shade in the shape if you were alone.
- **Step Three:** If you ate during a time you were bored, sad, anxious, worried, or experiencing any other negative emotion, put a circle around the circle so it looks like a bull's-eye, like this: ◉.
- **Step Four:** Continue working in this fashion until you have transferred each of your Food Diary entries onto the worksheet for the week.

Analysis

You can chart a full month's worth of Food Diary entries on the analysis worksheet. Looking at an entire month of entries can be especially revealing.

After each week and then for the month as a whole, consider the following:

- Can you see any trends between your mood and your food intake?
- What are the most challenging times of day for you to make healthy choices?
- How does being alone or being around others influence your choices?
- Do you tend to eat more frequently based on a specific mood?
- Is there a specific time of day you tend to eat more?

MONTH OF

Food Diary Analysis Worksheet

DATE → TIME ↓	1	2	3	4	5	6	7	8	9	10	11	12	13	14	15	16	17	18	19	20	21	22	23	24	25	26	27	28	29	30	31
5:00 AM																															
6:00 AM																															
7:00 AM																															
8:00 AM																															
9:00 AM																															
10:00 AM																															
11:00 AM																															
1200 PM																															
1:00 PM																															
2:00 PM																															
3:00 PM																															
4:00 PM																															
5:00 PM																															
6:00 PM																															
7:00 PM																															
8:00 PM																															
9:00 PM																															

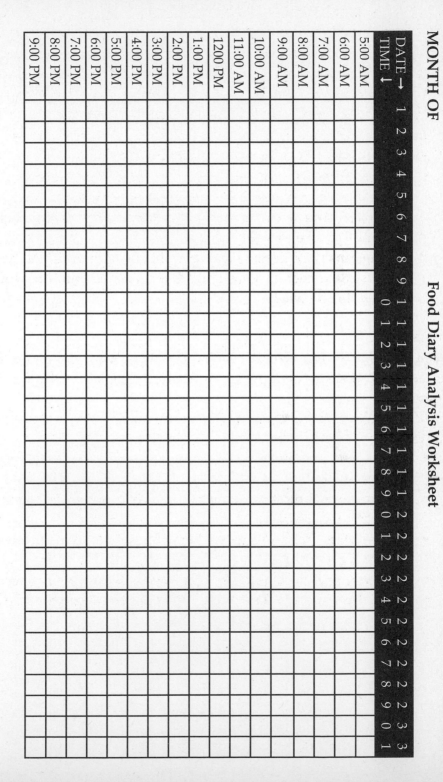

Three Simple Changes

These three simple techniques, when used regularly, can help you tackle the not-so-simple challenge of emotional and habitual eating. Each technique forces the association between food and mood or food and location to be challenged, which begins removing the "autopilot" eating patterns.

Mark Off the No-Food Zone

On the Food Diary Analysis worksheet, highlight the row containing the time you usually go to bed. Count back three hours, and draw a line across this row as shown in the example. This is the No-Food zone. <u>No matter what you eat, eat it outside of this zone</u>.

This simple change can help you lose weight and have more energy, as it will increase your metabolism and allow for better rest, because you are not digesting as much during the night. If you suffer from any gastrointestinal or reflux issues, this is a must. Remember, this change is not asking you to eat less; it is just asking you to <u>eat at a different time</u>.

Remember: Location, Location, Location

Look through your Food Diary and find the location where you ate the most frequently. If it was anywhere besides a table, make that location off-limits after lunchtime. Again, you are still free to eat what you like, but you must do it in a different location. This change is not asking you to eat less but to <u>eat in a different place</u>.

4:00 PM											
5:00 PM											
6:00 PM											
7:00 PM											
8:00 PM											
9:00 PM											
10:00 PM											
11:00 PM											

Mood and Food

Find the negative moods that influence unhealthy choices. List these moods on an index card.

Going forward, whenever you prepare to eat, make sure to identify your mood. If it is on this list — stop. Before you eat, take a ten-minute break to read something positive, write down affirmations, do your nails, put on your makeup, pet your pet, play a game of solitaire, or do anything else that is not emotionally draining. After ten minutes, you can choose to return to recording your mood and food, if you like. Often you will find that the urge to eat has passed, or if not, that you are able to make a healthier or more measured choice. This change is not asking you to eat less but to reflect before you eat.

My Three Simple Changes

On the reverse side of the index card where you listed your moods, write down the three changes you will make based on what you have learned. Keep this card with your Food Diary as a daily reminder.

mini-makeover
the caffeine culprit

"Caffeine produces a similar body pattern as stress. If you had a choice, how much stress would you consumer per day?"—*Brook Noel*

In this Mini you'll learn how caffeine affects both mind and body, how to tell if you are addicted, what the "safe levels" of caffeine are, when to avoid caffeine to maximize energy and emotional health, and how to create a realistic plan to curb or cut caffeine from your life.

Action Step Checklist
- ☐ Conduct a three-day inventory using the Caffeine-Tracking worksheet.
- ☐ Complete the caffeine-counting exercise.
- ☐ Complete the Caffeine Analysis and Taper worksheet.

Have you experienced any of the following within the past thirty days?
- ☐ Fatigue
- ☐ Mood swings
- ☐ Difficulty concentrating
- ☐ Performing under capability
- ☐ Impaired memory
- ☐ Anxiety

☐ Difficulty sleeping
☐ Jitteriness
☐ Headaches
☐ Anxiety
☐ Flushed face
☐ Nausea, diarrhea, or other gastrointestinal problems

These symptoms may be a result of your caffeine intake.

Nine out of ten Americans drink some sort of caffeinated beverage each day, making it the United States' number one "drug." Recent research also suggests a direct correlation between rising caffeine consumption and the need for both prescribed and over-the-counter sleep aids.

Just because the majority of us use caffeine doesn't change its effect on our brains, central nervous systems, and energy levels. In a nutshell, caffeine is manipulating the same channels in the brain as amphetamines and cocaine—but on a much milder basis. Understanding caffeine's influence on stress, sleep, anxiety, mood, and energy is important, especially since sleep and stress are *directly correlated* with many long-term physical ailments and emotional health issues. If you consume caffeine and also suffer from anxiety, stress, depression, mood swings, or fatigue, you might be surprised at caffeine's influence.

Caffeine Basics

In the brain, you have a neurotransmitter called adenosine. Adenosine is a relaxant that is necessary for the central nervous system to transition from stress to relaxation. Caffeine basically attaches to these areas and blocks the relaxing effects, resulting in a sustained feeling of arousal. Caffeine also encourages the release of cortisol, a hormone produced by stress.

> ***Think about it:*** *Caffeine produces a similar body pattern as stress. If you had a choice, how much stress would you consume per day?*

Caffeine also increases the body's levels of dopamine, the neurotransmitter related to pleasure. This explains why we experience moodiness and irritability when caffeine is suddenly removed from the system. This is a temporary condition; once your body regulates back to its natural state, it resumes normal, healthy function.

To recap:
- Caffeine blocks the reception of adenosine (associated with relaxation), creating a feeling of alertness.
- In individuals without adrenal impairment, this block of adenosine causes an increase in adrenaline.
- Dopamine levels are increased, creating a feeling of pleasure.

This at-a-glance view seems like the perfect solution for creating more energy! So what's the problem? Just like any drug, these effects wear off. When they do, they leave fatigue (and often depression) in their wake. How do we solve that? Bingo: we have some more caffeine.

People who have used caffeine for a long period of time may not feel this arousal or pleasure in the body. "I can drink any amount of caffeine," say some. While that may be true, this process is still occurring in your body. The difference is that you have developed a tolerance—meaning you are used to it.

Anyone who has ever had an alcoholic beverage might remember the effect of that very first drink. It doesn't take much to change the mental state of someone who is not used to alcohol. Yet over time, tolerance increases. Where one glass of wine might have altered your state before, now you can drink three. Does that mean only the third glass affects you? Of course not. The liver, kidneys, neurons—all still have to process the total, even if you aren't aware of it happening.

Three-Day Caffeine Inventory

Later in this Mini we will assess your caffeine-consumption habits and look at options should you choose to taper, refine, cut, or curb caffeine. In order to implement the later exercises fully, it is important to have an accurate assessment of your current caffeine intake. Photocopy as many copies of the Caffeine Tracking worksheet on the following page as necessary to track your caffeine consumption for the next three days, or print a full-size sheet from www. maketodaymatter.net.

Caffeine Tracking Worksheet

Time	What I Drank	Size	Amount of Caffeine

Each time you consume caffeine, write down the time, what you drank, the size (one can, one cup, sixteen ounces, etc.). Leave the last column blank for now. Make sure to record decaffeinated items as well, since many actually contain trace amounts of caffeine.

Caffeine and Energy

Caffeine interferes with sleep, even if you think it doesn't. Many people take a sleep aid to mask this problem. In fact, some doctors are starting to look intensely at caffeine usage before prescribing sleep aids (probably a very smart idea). In many cases, the problem isn't the inability to sleep; it is the inability to manage caffeine intake.

Caffeine has a half-life of six hours. Let's say you have a cup of coffee with 200 milligrams of caffeine at 3:30 p.m. At 9:30 p.m., 100 milligrams of that caffeine are still in your system. Caffeine keeps parts of the brain active that shouldn't be if we want to receive the full benefits of deep REM sleep. This solid sleep is incredibly vital to our health, mood, and energy. If you consume over 500 milligrams of caffeine a day or a large amount of caffeine within six hours of going to sleep, you are likely staring at your major energy problem.

Caffeine and sleep are the two biggest factors that we avoid addressing when we lack energy. Instead, we drink more caffeine to try and gain more energy and then wonder why we aren't well rested. Without the time to get more sleep, we just consume more caffeine and wonder why we have less and less energy over the years, often chalking it up as "I must be getting older."

The major symptoms of sleep deprivation are as follows:
- *Fatigue*
- *Mood swings*
- *Difficulty concentrating*
- *Performing under capability*
- *Impaired memory*

Caffeine itself is associated with several disorders:
- *Caffeine intoxication*
- *Caffeine-related anxiety disorder* *
- *Caffeine-related sleep disorder* *
- *Nausea, diarrhea, loose bowel, or other gastrointestinal problems*

***Those who take sleep medications and anxiety medications should definitely check their caffeine intake! There have been many cases where the cause of these issues was caffeine.*

** *Some initial studies are underway to evaluate whether the rise in irritable bowel syndrome (IBS) might be linked to the rise in caffeine consumption.*

Exercise: Counting Caffeine

Using the worksheets completed in your three-day inventory, look up how much caffeine you consumed in each beverage and then total each day. You can find the caffeine content of common beverages at the Mayo Clinic website: www.mayoclinic.com/health/caffeine/AN01211.

Breaking It Down by Numbers

Consuming more than 500 milligrams of caffeine per day is associated with dependence—meaning you may experience withdrawal symptoms. Some research puts that number as high as 1,000 milligrams, but the majority of studies are in agreement that 500 milligrams is a good general guideline.

To Curb or to Cut?

With caffeine being an addictive substance, it stands to reason that the faster you eliminate caffeine, the greater the withdrawal symptoms.

If you have strong willpower and want to go "cold turkey," go for it! The chance of relapse is high during the first seven days; therefore I personally advocate a taper over time. Those who taper over time will experience the side effects at a less noticeable rate.

Time Course of Caffeine Withdrawal

Caffeine-withdrawal symptoms follow an orderly course. According to a study from Johns Hopkins University, onset usually occurs twelve to twenty-four hours after terminating caffeine intake, although onset as late as thirty-six hours has been documented. Peak withdrawal intensity has generally been described as occurring twenty to forty-eight hours after abstinence. The duration of withdrawal has most often been described as ranging from two days to one week.

What symptoms should you expect if you go cold turkey? Headaches, fatigue, dizziness, lack of focus, irritability, and anxiety are common. You have the choice of going cold turkey and trying to "grin and bear it" for four to seven days, or you can taper over time. I personally chose to taper over time, as I did not (and still do not) have any desire to eliminate caffeine from my diet completely.

A note about treating the headache: Be careful about using pain relievers to soothe caffeine-withdrawal headaches. Some pain relievers contain caffeine. The reason they work is that they do the very same thing as caffeine: constrict blood vessels. Caffeine-withdrawal headaches are caused by the resumed normal flow of blood vessels. So if you take a pain reliever that contains caffeine, you are still consuming caffeine. Once the body adjusts back to its normal, healthy tendency, these headaches stop.

As an alternative and at the suggestion of a massage therapist, I purchased a U-shaped pillow that fits around the neck. Composed of an interior bag and a cover, the bag can be placed in the freezer. (You can also heat these in the microwave; just remember heat increases blood flow—not what you want during caffeine withdrawal but great once you are past it and seeking relaxation.) I had two of these pillows, so one was always frozen. At night I would put one around my neck before going to sleep.

The ice reduces the blood flow naturally and works as a shorter-term fix than consuming caffeinated pain relievers. I tried noncaffeinated pain medicines, but they did not help. This ice technique has become one I use for most tension headaches.

You can create a similar solution by using a sturdy zip-top gallon-size freezer bag. Place crushed ice in the bag (it needs to be finely crushed to be comfortable and conform to the neck), or freeze a bag of beans. Wrap either in a soft towel before applying (never place ice directly against skin).

Creating a Caffeine-Taper Plan

If you decide to follow a caffeine-taper plan, here are some guidelines:

- Determine how much caffeine you are actually consuming. Use the link provided earlier along with your caffeine-inventory worksheet.
- Complete the Caffeine Analysis and Taper worksheet. Put your average morning wake-up time at the top of the left column. Then list each hour of the day until you have gone all the way through to your waking time. For example, if you wake up at 6:00 a.m., place that in the first

blank, 7:00 a.m. in the next, 8:00 a.m. in the next, etc., and keep going until you hit 5:00 a.m.

- Place a line or star next to or highlight the hour in which you usually go to sleep. Count back three hours before that, and mark those areas with a D. From D count three more hours back, and mark these areas with a C. From C count two hours back, and mark this area B. Any other waking hours become area A.

Caffeine Analysis and Taper Worksheet

Wake Time	Hour(s) from Wake Time	Area (A, B, C, D)	Average Consumption	Taper Goal
	1			
	2			
	3			
	4			
	5			
	6			
	7			
	8			
	9			
	10			
	11			
	12			
	13			
	14			
	15			
	16			
	17			
	18			
	19			
	20			
	21			
	22			
	23			
	24			

> *Tip:* Refer to my sample in this section as a guide.

Figure out how much caffeine you average during these periods using the three-day inventory you completed at the start of this lesson. Write this number in the Average Consumption column.

- **Phase One:** The first goal is to eliminate consumption of caffeine in the D area. The good news is that, biologically, this is the easiest area in which to reduce caffeine. Our circadian rhythms prompt us to begin "shutting down" in the early evening. (In the morning, our circadian rhythm desires wakefulness, which is why caffeine cravings are greatest upon waking.) Your body doesn't store caffeine, but it takes many hours to excrete it; therefore reducing consumption closest to bedtime makes the greatest impact in improving your quality of sleep.

> *Tip:* I recommend fully completing phase one before moving on to phase two.

- **Phase Two:** Take a look at your average consumption during periods B and C. Ideally, you would not have any caffeine in areas B, C, or D to ensure caffeine has left your system before sleep. For now, however, work to <u>limit</u> your consumption during periods B and C to 100–200 milligrams. I say limit because somewhere in here the body is at its "lowest" point of the day (besides when sleeping—but we will discuss this more later). If you are drinking a lot of caffeine, cutting off these areas will be difficult; it is better to curb some consumption in area A.

Tip: I recommend fully completing phase two before moving on to phase three.

- **Phase Three:** Subtract the milligrams you consume during periods B and C from 500. (This assumes you are not consuming any caffeine in period D.) The amount left over is your personal guideline for maximum consumption in period A. For example, I drink around 400 to 500 milligrams per day (a little more than the recommended guideline of 200 to 300 milligrams, but it does seem to work for my body). I drink all except 100 to 200 milligrams in the first period upon waking; I save that last 100 to 200 milligrams for early afternoon.

So How Long Does This Take?

As long as you need it to in order to be successful. Remember, progress—not perfection. If you tremble at the thought of reducing caffeine, start slowly. Make a new goal each week. You don't have to do this in a short period of time.

Special Considerations

Some antibiotics and medications can increase the length of time caffeine stays in your body, which can amplify caffeine side effects. Antibiotics are the most common medication in this family.

The other big culprit is ma huang (commonly called ephedra), which has been banned as an herbal supplement by the Food and Drug Administration; however, it can still be found in some herbal teas. Make sure to check your labels!

If you are taking medication or have specific health conditions, talk to your doctor about any unique caffeine recommendations.

Brook's Sample

Caffeine Analysis and Taper Worksheet

Wake Time	Hour(s) from Wake Time	Area (A, B, C, D)	Average Consumption	Taper Goal
4:30 a.m.	1	A	300 mg of caffeine	
5:30 a.m.	2	A		
6:30 a.m.	3	A		
7:30 a.m.	4	A		
8:30 a.m.	5	A		
9:30 a.m.	6	A		
10:30 a.m.	7	A		
11:30 a.m.	8	A		
12:30 p.m.	9	A		
1:30 p.m.	10	A	100–200 mg of caffeine somewhere in here	
2:30 p.m.	11	B		
3:30 p.m.	12	B		
4:30 p.m.	13	C		
5:30 p.m.	14	C		
6:30 p.m.	15	C		
7:30 p.m.	16	D		
8:30 p.m.	17	D		
9:30 p.m.	18	D		
10:30 p.m.	19	Lights out 10:30		
11:30 p.m.	20			
12:30 a.m.	21			
1:30 a.m.	22			
2:30 a.m.	23			
3:30 a.m.	24			

mini-makeover

nine steps to breaking a bad habit

"If we can create a bad habit, then we also have the power to uncreate it."
—*Brook Noel*

Habits are not formed overnight but through repetition. Each time we repeat a behavior, whether positive or negative, we strengthen neuroconnectors in the brain. Fortunately, science has shown that we can "rewire" our connectors and thus rewire our habits. In this Mini I'll walk you through the science of breaking a bad habit. Taking deliberate action on each step over a realistic period of time will be the key to freeing your life of negative habits.

Action Step Checklist

- ☐ Complete the first four questions on the Habit worksheet.
- ☐ Complete the background question on the Habit worksheet.
- ☐ Finish completing the Habit worksheet.
- ☐ Track your habit for one week.
- ☐ Define your obstacles.
- ☐ Chart your steps toward change.
- ☐ Decide if you will use the Advanced Tracking worksheet, and if so, print a copy as you begin your journey!

Almost everyone has some habit that steals a little (or a lot) of joy from day-to-day life. Sometimes the habits are obvious: overeating, procrastinating, overspending, drinking too much caffeine, smoking. Other times they are less obvious, like avoiding health-enhancing behaviors (such as exercise), making excuses, spending too much time on the computer, blaming others, getting angry quickly, not taking care of ourselves—just to name a few.

Over time the word "habit" can become synonymous with "excuse." We begin to feel that we cannot change an area because it is a habit, and stereotypically, habits are hard to break. However, if we have the power to create a habit, then we also have the power to uncreate it. How do we know if a habit needs to be broken? When it begins to negatively impact our relationships, self-esteem, finances, career, or any other area important to us, then a habit has become a hurt.

Breaking a habit takes focus, awareness, and intention, since we need to turn off the "autopilot" we have developed and make deliberate, new choices.

Analyzing the Habit

Although you may have several habits you would like to change, because of the time, energy, and focus involved, choose one habit to focus on first. Attempting to change multiple habits at once is a common reason people fail. Think about those who make five lofty resolutions at the start of a new year. It is hard to keep one, let alone five! Our busy lives and schedules demand much of our focus, and we need to target the remaining focus toward a single area in which change is desired. I have found people increase their odds of success by starting with the least intimidating habit on their list. By working through an "easier" habit, we gain strength and confidence in our ability to break through habits' barriers.

Clearly Define Your Habit and Its Purpose
We don't create negative habits for fun and to purposely complicate our lives. We create a habit because, *at the time of creation, it seems*

to serve a purpose in our lives. Typically we outgrow the need for the behavior—but we don't relinquish the habit. Most often these habits seem to offer a short-term benefit that makes them an easy choice in a busy or complicated day.

The first step in breaking a bad habit is to clearly answer each of these questions:

- What is the habit?
- When did I start engaging in this habit?
- How long have I been engaging in this habit?
- What purpose does this habit serve? What does it help me avoid?

We can't mange or change what we do not clearly understand, so taking some time to soul search for the habit's origins gives us a framework for future change. Use the Habit worksheet to answer these questions. Make sure to give each some thought: the more thorough your answers, the more solid your foundation will be.

Gather Some Basic Background

Take a quick inventory of the past twelve months. Answer the following questions:

- How much time did you spend keeping up this habit?
- How much did this habit cost you financially?
- What did this habit cost you emotionally?
- What did this habit prevent you from doing?

Answering these questions can help you clearly see the effect of a particular habit in your life.

Habit Worksheet

What is the habit? _____

When did I start engaging in this habit? _____

How long have I been engaging in this habit? _____

What purpose does this habit serve? What does it help me avoid? _____
_____
_____

Background:

How much time do I spend keeping up this habit?
_____
_____

How much does this habit cost me financially?
_____
_____

What does this habit cost me emotionally?
_____
_____

What does this habit prevent me from doing?
_____
_____

Breaking this habit is important because
_____
_____
_____

Common Denominators:

Physical: _____
_____

Emotional: _____
_____

Substitute List:
_____
_____

Support Team: (include name, email, phone)
_____
_____

Fast-Forward
As you conduct your habit analysis, imagine what your days would be like if you were rid of this habit. What would change? Write about how your life would be different. Write as much as you can about the benefits of changing your ways. Try to come up with at least ten separate reasons for change. The more you think through the benefits (and write them down), the more solid the foundation you will have when you begin to implement change.

Track Your Habit
Print several copies of the Habit worksheet, and for the next week, write down each time you engage in your habit. Note anything that might be influencing you, such as those around you or how you feel emotionally or physically. Conducting this "habit audit" offers insight into exactly how a habit is surfacing and affecting day-to-day activities.

Finding the Common Denominators
All habits have environmental factors that enable them to take place. Some are obvious: overeating requires an environment with food indulgences; spending too much time on the computer requires a computer.

Others are related to specific environments or activities. For example, smoking can be associated with a specific desk, room, time, or accompaniment, like coffee.

Other habits, such as procrastinating, are characterized by "avoidance environments." For example, instead of exercising, one might watch television, or instead of working on a project, a person might get sidetracked by the Internet.

What are the common denominators in your habit environment?

_____

_____

_____

_____

Emotional Common Denominators
Harder to detect but present nonetheless, emotional common denominators are the perceived emotional gains derived from engaging in a habit. Usually these involve a perceived instant gratification and are often related to mood. For example, the over-eating of sweets produces increased dopamine levels in the brain (dopamine is associated with happiness). A cigarette may be a way of relieving stress, worry, or anxiety. Procrastinating might offer a more pleasurable short-term task while we avoid something more challenging.

Look through your Habit Inventory and see if you can detect the emotional common denominators surrounding your habit.

Breaking a Habit's Hold

There are two approaches to breaking a habit. The first is the "cold turkey" approach in which a person immediately ceases the habit without a cessation process. The second involves changing the behaviors and environmental factors that surround the habit, and in time the habit naturally resolves itself.

I have found the second approach to yield better long-term results. The all-or-nothing approach often creates pressure and anxiety that causes people to stall in getting started or, if they do start, relapse soon after.

If you wish to try the cold turkey approach, skip to the next section. If you wish to try the cessation approach, continue with this section, and follow these Nine Steps to break your habit.

Step One: Change the Environment
Revisit the environmental influences you uncovered. What environmental changes can you make that would help reduce the hold of the habit? Often people engage in habits while engaging in a second activity—for example, eating while watching television or working at the computer. If you can relate, try choosing a different location (like the dining room table), and avoid multitasking so all of your focus is on the habit itself. This helps turn off "autopilot."

Step Two: Delay — Don't Deprive

Begin putting a distance between impulse and action. If you have the impulse to eat, wait five minutes before eating. If you have the impulse to procrastinate, act for five minutes before putting the project aside. Each week add five minutes to this delay between impulse and action.

Step Three: Turn Off Autopilot

Each time you engage in the habit, make sure to write it down prior to engagement. For example, if you are trying to break the cigarette cycle, before lighting up, write down the time and date, and complete this sentence: "I am going to have a cigarette at ____." Many people find that habits done without thinking are greatly reduced by this simple observation.

Step Four: Create a Substitute List

The best tool for breaking an existing habit is springing into action. Creating a list of activities you can do instead of your habit will help you avoid the "think tank" — without a substitute activity, your mind will wander toward your habit and increase your compulsion to engage. Since the mind cannot think about two things at once, it makes sense that engaging in another activity will reduce its focus on the habit.

Look at the list of emotions associated with your habit. Use the substitute list on the Habit worksheet to brainstorm alternative activities that could help with the emotions fueling your habit. Place this list near the environment associated with your habit. For example, if you are working on reducing eating, place the list on the fridge. If you are working to reduce spending, fold it to fit in your wallet.

Step Five: Make a Commitment

After you have completed the previous steps, it is time to clearly define what you want to change and how you want to change it. Make a detailed plan by breaking down the steps you need to take. It would be a bit unrealistic to say that in four weeks you will never overspend if you have been overspending for years. Dramatic overhauls often lead to slips and relapses. Try creating a multitiered plan for change: choose and define your new goal; then set milestones between where you are currently and where you would like to be. If you routinely overspend a hundred dollars a week, you could reduce your spending by twenty dollars every other week, and in two months you would have a twenty-dollar spending budget each week. Write down your steps on a calendar, making sure to include specifics and dates, or use the Steps toward Change worksheet on page 66.

Overcoming Obstacles

Obstacle	Solution

Step Six: Think It Through

Before your start date, think through the challenges you are likely to face: What might confuse you? What might cause you to run from new change? What might cause you to slip? Think of as many potential roadblocks as you can and write them down. On your own or with the help of others, brainstorm a solution for each of these roadblocks and write them on the Overcoming Obstacles worksheet.

Step Seven: Tell Someone!

Once you have defined the change you want to make and chosen the steps to take, commit to a start date—and tell someone what you are doing! None of us like to go back on our word. If we don't tell anyone about the change we are contemplating, it is easy to revamp and alter the plan at any time. If we share our goals with others and ask them to help us be accountable, we are much more likely to succeed.

Step Eight: Begin!

When your start date arrives, review your plan. On a daily basis, review the reasons for change that you listed at the start of this Mini. Rely on your support person or group for help when needed. If you find new roadblocks, do not abandon your plan. Instead, add them to the list of obstacles you created in Step Six and continue brainstorming solutions on your own or with your support person or group.

Step Nine: Don't Let a Slip Become a Fall

Often we have a little slip (or a big one), and that becomes a reason to abandon our plan altogether. Don't! Just because you slipped today doesn't mean you need to slip tomorrow. Don't let the shame of one setback be a reason to abandon your plan. Instead, add that as a roadblock and brainstorm a solution for the next time you face that specific scenario. Take the day off, and then get back on track tomorrow!

Steps toward Change

Month	Day	I will have accomplished	Complete

household management & maintenance

When our homes are out of control or in disarray, it can quickly take its toll on our sense of inner peace and well-being. In this section we explore some ways to streamline household management for daily activities like cooking, cosmetics, and managing your wardrobe.

Mini-Makeovers
- Simplifying Your Wardrobe
- Creating a Recipe Library
- Mastering Meal Planning
- Controlling Your Cosmetics
- Beautifying Your Home
- Responsibilities and Rewards

mini-makeover

simplifying your wardrobe

"The finest clothing made is a person's skin, but, of course, society demands something more than this."—*Mark Twain*

Every year women spend countless hours putting on and taking off, folding and unfolding, carrying up, down, and around, and searching for clothing. Then there are the wardrobe-maintenance tasks, like dry-cleaning trips, mending, ironing, soaking, taking something off in frustration and then adding it to a pile we later have to fold. Often the simple task of dressing becomes a source of stress and lost time. It also influences a person's attitude. Who wants to begin her morning by putting on an outfit and deciding, "I don't like how this looks!" In this Mini I'll walk you through a wardrobe makeover, with four weekly assignments.

Action Step Checklist
- ☐ Collect all of your clothes.
- ☐ If you are behind on laundry, use the catch-up routine.
- ☐ Gather all clothing items into one location.
- ☐ Sort all clothing into one of three piles: Favorite Outfits, Homeless Favorites, or Not Favorites.
- ☐ Asses your closet personality using the tips in this Mini.
- ☐ Reassemble your closet using the provided guidelines.

In the past ninety days, have you

- put on a top or bottom that you liked, only to realize you did not have a matching top or bottom to wear with it, and thus changed your complete outfit?
- tried on more than two outfits for a single event?
- tried on a piece of clothing, only to discover you no longer liked the way it looked—but left it in your closet anyway?
- went to wear a specific item and discovered it needed to be mended, ironed, or dry-cleaned?
- discovered a pile of clothes that needs repairing, ironing, or dry-cleaning but has not moved forward in any of the aforementioned processes in the last three weeks?

The more questions you answered with a yes, the more this Mini will help you to simplify your wardrobe and create a smooth and stress-free routine.

Week One: Collecting Your Clothing and Clearing Out Clutter

To make a closet functional, the first step is to make sure the most accessible space contains only the clothing we need (and want) to access. Whenever I work with someone on a closet, the first thing I do is clear out the clothing clutter—items that might be absolutely wonderful but are rarely worn because they are (1) the wrong size, (2) only worn for special occasions, (3) in need of ironing, mending, or other maintenance, (4) off-season (will someone living in Wisconsin really wear shorts and a tank top when it is twenty degrees below outside?), or (5) not relevant, like maternity clothing for a woman who is not pregnant yet but is saving the items for her next pregnancy.

Often I find prime closet space is filled with rarely worn items, making it challenging to find desired items. If our closets aren't organized effectively, before we know it items are strewn everywhere as we hunt for a specific shirt or pair of pants.

Take any items that meet these qualifications for clothing clutter, and choose one of these options to apply:

1.   Move rarely worn items into a separate closet.
2.   If items are foldable, place them in a plastic tub, label it, and store it out of the way. (If items are delicate, like sweaters, consider storing in plastic clothing-storage bags before placing in tub.)
3.   Use one of the other storage strategies that will be covered in week three.

Brook's Catch-Up Routine
(for those who don't get along with laundry)

Since we are applying this to our own wardrobes, focus on your clothing first. You can come back and use this same technique to conquer other family members' wardrobes afterward.

- *Today or tonight, gather all of your clothing that needs washing. Separate this from other family members' clothing, towels, etc.*
- *Start a load in the washer before you go to sleep.*
- *Tomorrow morning transfer the washed clothes to the dryer. Place a new load in the washer.*
- *Tomorrow night fold the load from the dryer, transfer the clothing in the washer to the dryer, and start a new load in the washer before going to bed.*
- *Repeat daily until you are caught up on your laundry.*

Gather the Goods

After identifying and relocating clutter, it is time to gather everything you have to work with into one place. Don't worry about folding, putting away, or storing items at this stage of the game. (Later, when we discuss storage, you may want to change your closet organization, so putting things away is not important right now.) Instead, focus on washing, dry-cleaning, ironing, or repairing any clothing in need and then corralling all of your clothing toward your closet.

- If you are behind on laundry, get caught up on washing *your* clothing first (see Brook's Catch-Up Routine). Take in any items that need dry-cleaning to the dry-cleaner early in the week so you can pick them up at week's end.

- Mend or repair anything that needs mending (hems, buttons, etc.).
- Iron anything that needs ironing.

Week Two: Sorting

With your clothing accounted for, it is time to create three categories:

1. **Favorite Outfits:** This clothing makes you feel good, is comfortable, and matches. For example, you have a favorite sweater and a skirt or pants to go with it.
2. **Homeless Favorites:** This clothing also makes you feel good and is comfortable, yet it is missing a match. For example you have a sweater you love—but you don't have a skirt or pants you love to go with it.
3. **Not Favorites:** You don't love it, but you wear it.

This week we want to focus on the first two categories: Favorite Outfits and Homeless Favorites. The goal here is to make sure "no favorites are left behind. "Work systematically from one end of your closet to the other and then one drawer at a time, removing favorite items. Place them into one of two categories: Favorite Outfits or Homeless Favorites. When you are done, you should have two categories of clothing.

The Count
Count how many outfits you have in the Favorite Outfits category. Write the number on the Simplify Your Wardrobe worksheet.

The Down and Dirty Facts
How often do you do *your* laundry? Do you wash *your* items once a week, twice a week? Do you do laundry every other week? Some people do laundry every day, but they are washing other people's items, not their own. What we are looking for is a realistic estimate of how often *your personal clothing* makes it through the laundry cycle. (By the way, there is not a "correct" answer. Don't be fooled that you "should" do a laundry X times per week. One of my closest

friends is married without kids, and she does laundry twice a month. This routine works fine for her family, because she and her husband have enough clothes to last that long. Then she tackles it all in one day. I have another single friend who runs a load every other day, washing her two outfits, towels, everything.) Write in your laundry frequency on the worksheet.

The Reality

Compare the two numbers. Do you have enough favorite outfits to match your laundry schedule? For example, if you run personal laundry once a week, do you have seven combos in your favorite group?

While you might run personal laundry every three to four days, few people want to wear the same three or four outfits over and over. People have asked me what I think a good number of "combos" is to have at the ready. I have personally found ten to be my magic number. I have ten home combos, ten work combos, and then four church combos. If you live in a seasonal area like I do, then to adapt my system, you would have ten combos for summer work, ten for winter work, etc. I have found no matter how many outfits I have, I tend to wear the same set of clothing again and again. I find clothing is a lot like kids' toys: it goes in phases. If you have tons of favorites, narrow it down to no more than fifteen combos you are wearing the most *right now*. When you get bored or want a change, switch them out.

If you find that you have enough outfits to get through between laundries, then you have discovered your core wardrobe and are ready to proceed to the next section.

Special Considerations and Tips

Too many clothes? There is one other important guideline for scaling back if you have too many favorite combos: are they easy to maintain? In other words if they require dry cleaning or ironing, do you have a system in place for dry-cleaning or ironing that makes them easy to maintain? I have a dry-cleaning routine in place, but ironing and I will never get along—and I am okay with that now. I used to hold on to clothing in need of ironing just in case one day I became magically inspired to take up the sport. After five years of anti-ironing, I can safely assume it isn't happening. Since this realization, I have not purchased one item that needs ironing.

Separate work wardrobe? If you have separate work clothes, then you would apply this same procedure to work clothes. The only change is that when you put items back into the closet (which we'll cover next), you should maintain two separate areas. All clothing pertaining to work should be in one section and all clothing for off-days in another section. If you have two separate hanging rods, then this is easy. If not, use a decorated hanger to divide work clothes from non-work clothes.

Short on favorites? If you are short on favorite combos, revisit the pile we set aside earlier—Homeless Favorites, a.k.a. favorites without matches. Look through the Not Favorite group (clothes you don't love but wear), and see if you can find a temporary solution. Then write down what you would need ideally to complete this combo. For example, I have a sweater I love, but when I completed this exercise, I discovered I really didn't have the right match for it. (This explains why I haven't worn it in quite some time.) While I could wear it with jeans, that option doesn't give me the same feeling as my other favorite combos. A pair of dark brown slacks would be a better match. But alas, I don't have any, so I added "brown slacks" to the Items Needed section of the Simplify Your Wardrobe worksheet. Go through your other stray favorites; determine what you would need to make this outfit a favorite combo, and add it to the items needed list. Create combos with what you have as you work to attain the items on this list, and be on the lookout for good deals on the ones you need.

As you create a new combo you love, replace one of your Not Favorite outfits.

Week Three: Configuring Your Closet

The favorite combos collected in the last section are like Broadway and Park Place in Monopoly—prime real estate. We need to find an appropriate "prime real estate" area in your closet. Determine what area is most accessible and useable *for you*, and place favorite combos there.

A couple of guidelines: First, if you have seasonal combos, place the current season's combos in the prime real estate space. Put the others with your special occasion wear, and you can swap out seasonally. I have found this to be a good practice to avoid having to dig for something or having items get mixed up. Plus, by the time the next season comes, I have usually forgotten what I have, and uncovering these favorites feels like Christmas.

Second, make sure your storage choices match your closet personality practices.

What's Your Closet Personality?
There are two basic types of closet personalities: Hangers and Pilers. Pilers have two variations:
- **The Organized Piler:** This Piler has items folded and neatly placed on shelves, in dressers, or in wardrobes.
- **The Perpetual Piler:** The Perpetual Piler has clothes strewn on chairs, floors, and shelves that rarely make it to hangers. Often the only time a Piler's clothing sees a hanger is when he or she does a "big clean." Then, three weeks later (or sooner), it is back in a pile. You can tell you are a Piler if you look to a pile to get dressed in the morning instead of a closet rod. (Often the Perpetual Piler's clean clothes live folded in a laundry basket on a closet floor, waiting to be worn.)

Hanger personalities have a more organized approach to clothing. Usually they have at least several special hangers in their closet— like skirts hangers, slacks hangers, or special wooden hangers. When Hanger personalities go to get dressed, they usually select items from hangers.

Closet Compatibility and Creative Storage
It is important for a closet to provide storage solutions compatible with your clothing personality, or any organizational attempt will

be short lived. I am a Perpetual Piler. I have a big walk-in closet and plenty of hanging-rod space. Since that is the space I had, for many years I tried to put everything on hangers. As you might guess, it didn't take long for the piles to return.

Since I don't purchase clothing that requires ironing and even my dressy clothes are from a wrinkle-free, wash-and-wear collection, I have little use for hanging space. I do like to hang my hoodies and jackets so I can grab them quickly (I am always wearing layers), but I have never much cared for clothes hangers. I always joke that my hangers end up in a gnarled tangle that would require expert yoga flexibility to undo!

I finally realized that while I had a large closet space, it was not workable space for me.

I looked at my inventoried clothing and decided to make my closet compatible. I didn't have the budget to install a full system like a California closet, so I chose creativity instead. I added additional shelving and used crates to make space for more folded items. I removed one rod altogether and mounted pegboard on the now exposed wall. I purchased the pegboard inexpensively at Home Depot and then purchased rubber-ended hooks. I use these hooks for my sweaters, hoodies, and jackets. When I cut the pegboard to size, I had a leftover strip about two inches tall by three feet wide. I mounted that in my closet and added hooks to hang necklaces.

I left the other hanging rod in the closet, but since I did not use the full length of it, I transformed the unused space into workable storage by adding a sweater bag with two hooks intended to hang on a closet rod. The sweater bag has eight compartments, and I use it to hold my T-shirts.

All of these storage ideas came from my asking one simple question: *What would work for me?* Consider this question for yourself; the possibilities are limitless.

If you prefer hanging items in your closet, consider the pegboard technique to maximize otherwise unused space. Also, many closets have one closet rod at eye level. If this is the case, consider adding a second rod at waist height to increase storage.

If you don't have all the supplies you need right now, that's okay—I didn't either. Work with what you have on hand. Add other items to the notes section of the Simplify Your Wardrobe worksheet. This week work on making your closet compatible with your personality.

Week Four: Reassembling Your Closet

With your closet configured, it is time to put items away. Remember to put your favorite combos in the most accessible place. If you share a closet, consider a separate laundry basket or hamper to keep all of your clothes together.

The Leftovers: Not Favorites

Stand and look at the nice combos you put together. Imagine going to dress and having this simple set of options waiting for you. Now look at the last pile of items you don't love but wear: the Not Favorites. Do you really want or need to keep the contents? Do you want the clutter?

I found that I liked the simplicity of knowing each outfit I put on made me feel good. I took everything else to a woman's shelter—eighteen bags of clothes, shoes, belts, and miscellaneous. At first I felt a bit guilty, like I was wasting money by not keeping these items I had purchased. Then I realized the only waste was to let this clothing sit in my closet unworn.

It felt great to walk into my closet the next morning. No searching. No debating. No trying something on and then throwing it into a pile. I loved everything there.

If you aren't ready to stomach the big giveaway, then please do this: Package all the clothing in bags or boxes and either store it out of the way or stack it in the closet. Live with your simple wardrobe for the next thirty days. Then come back and see if you are ready for the big giveaway.

> *Trade Up Tip: Take your Not Favorite items — or any clothing you don't wear at all — to a local consignment shop to resell, or hold a garage sale.*
>
> *Use that money to finance your items-needed list or buy accessories for the favorites you do have. If you are still low on favorite combos, don't despair! I have completed this exercise with women who had only two or three combos they really loved. However, after applying some savings strategies, they were able to build more favorites over time. Many found not having enough favorites was a blessing in disguise, because they were able to buy "on purpose" instead of "on impulse."*

Maintaining Your System

As you buy new clothes or add new items, make sure to remove anything you like less. Once a year, review these steps to freshen your wardrobe.

Shopping Tips

When clothes shopping, it is very important to be in the right mind-set. You want to go on a day where you are not pressed for time and can try on everything (even T-shirts)! Everything fits everyone differently. If you prefer to catalog shop, make sure the store provides a no-hassle return system.

If you are looking for a match to a favorite item, make sure to either wear the favorite item the day you shop or take it with you. Try the whole outfit on at the store to avoid ending up with another wear-it-but-don't-love-it item.

As you purchase clothes, make sure to replace the items you don't love to keep your wardrobe current and functional.

Look for fabrics that match your closet personality. If you know you will not iron, then look for wrinkle-free items. If you rarely go to the dry-cleaner, avoid items that need dry-cleaning.

Keep your items-needed list with you so that you can buy on purpose instead of on impulse. Watch for sales and good deals on the items on this list.

Simplify Your Wardrobe Worksheet

Total Number of Favorites: _____

Laundry Frequency: _____

My Goal Number of Favorite Combos: _____

Items Needed:

_____

_____

_____

_____

_____

_____

_____

_____

_____

_____

_____

_____

_____

_____

_____

_____

_____

_____

_____

Notes (favorite fabrics, sizes, etc.):

_____

_____

_____

_____

_____

_____

mini-makeover

creating a recipe library

"One of the very nicest things about life is the way we must regularly stop whatever we are doing and devote our attention to eating."
—*Luciano Pavarotti*

Because recipes are timeless, it can be hard to trim back on recipe magazines and cookbooks. After all, the recipes in *Cooking Light* will taste just as good ten years from now as they will today. You have likely heard the cliché "too many cooks in the kitchen." The same can be said for recipes: if we have too many recipes, it can be difficult to find what we need when we need it, or we may be taking up tons of space with recipes we will never prepare, making the "golden nuggets" hard to find. In this Mini I'll share how to cull your collection into a customized cookbook of culinary favorites.

Action Step Checklist
- ☐ Read up to Step One.
- ☐ Gather necessary supplies.
- ☐ Complete the reading and Create Your Cooking Criteria activity.
- ☐ Find a recipe magazine and read Create Your Cooking Criteria and Cut and Categorize.
- ☐ Begin creating your categories following the instructions in Cut and Categorize. (I recommend cutting and pasting from at least one or two magazines before creating categories. This will give you a better idea of what categories you need to begin with.)
- ☐ Read the section on maintenance and indexing.
- ☐ Maintain your library.

> *Tip:* If you plan to work through the Mastering Meal Planning Mini, I recommend working through this Mini first.

Note: This process took me a long time, as I had many, many, many cookbooks. However, it combined several of my favorite activities: scrapbooking, organizing, paging through magazines, and food. I found this to be a great activity to work on while watching television or a movie or just relaxing. Instead of setting out to complete your library in a month, enjoy the process. (I often clipped articles or recipes to send to friends as well.) Aim to spend a certain amount of time each week, or work through a specific number of magazines or cookbooks each month.

If you are reading these pages, I am guessing at least one of the following statements is true:

- You have more than ten cookbooks.
- You have more than twenty cookbooks.
- You have so many cookbooks you aren't sure.
- You have many recipe magazines.
- You have many recipe magazines that you have not cooked from.
- You have a large collection of personal recipes.
- You have a stack of recipes saved in your email inbox or printed from the Internet to try.

In 2004 I was struggling to find "that one chicken recipe" I remembered making in Portland. The recipe had come up in a random conversation, and my family desperately wanted me to make it again. I said, "Sure! I loved that recipe, too!" Then, as I ran from one pile of cookbooks to another, I realized I had no clue where it was.

The "chicken recipe" identifier wasn't very helpful—I had four thick books filled with only chicken recipes! And who is to say it would be in one of those? My daughter offered, "I think you found it in *Cooking Light*." I was hopeful for about three minutes, at which point I uncovered three *Cooking Light* anthologies and three years of monthly magazines. As I paged through book after book in search of the infamous "chicken recipe," I realized just how many of the pages I turned contained recipes my family would not eat.It was then and there I decided to transform my chaotic cookbook collection into an efficient, usable recipe library.

This Mini will walk you through the steps I took to trim down my collection to be functional and friendly and show you how to do the same.

Supply List

- Scissors
- Glue stick or transparent tape
- Three-ring binder with lined or blank paper inside (you may need more than one)
- Write-on tabs to fit the three-ring binder (a pack of eight or ten should do)
- Three-hole-punched paper — choose either white card stock, plain white paper (which comes pre-punched at office stores), or regular school-notebook paper that is three-hole punched

Optional but suggested:
- Clear page protectors — add a few in the front page of the binder (when you choose a recipe to cook from, place it into the protector sheet and remove it from the binder; this will protect your recipe page from spills and drips if you are a "creative" chef)

Depending on how many recipes you have, you will likely want to add additional binders and tabs. However, start with one. This will allow you to determine exactly what you need and avoid overbuying and overcomplicating the process.

Step One: Create Your Cooking Criteria

Before you begin browsing cookbooks and magazines, consider the criteria for your master cooking library. You want to make sure to keep this soon-to-be-customized cookbook user friendly.

I have the criteria I use printed on a sheet of paper and placed on the inside cover of my binder to guide my collection building.

Master Recipe Collection Qualifications

Does it match my diet? If I am on a low-sodium diet, I can drastically reduce the number of recipes that would be considered for reference.

Would I actually make this? Yes, the Moroccan salmon cakes with garlic mayonnaise and the vanilla crème brûlee with raspberry sauce look delectable, but would I actually make them?

Do I even like this? I don't like tuna—end of story. All tuna recipes go.

Do I already have a "favorite" recipe for this? If I already have a family-favorite sloppy joe or barbecue chicken recipe, then I don't need another one. Finding a family-approved recipe isn't easy. Follow the cliché "If it ain't broke, don't fix it."

How many sugar cookie recipes does one person need? If I were to save every good-looking sugar cookie recipe I found, I would have well over a hundred. Given that I bake cookies once a year, that doesn't seem too practical.

How often do we eat this course? Our family is not big on dessert. When we do have dessert, it is usually a treat from a local ice cream parlor. (Keeping ice cream or chocolate in the house is just too tempting!) If I were to count the desserts I actually made last year— well, actually, I didn't make any. My husband made a traditional family recipe that we have every Christmas. During the holidays, I cooked the main courses and sides, and relatives brought the desserts. Desserts are my "slimmest" category. (How often can you use "slim" and "dessert" in the same sentence?) Breakfast is another course to consider: how often do you make a strata or French toast casserole? While this doesn't mean you can't keep any recipes for this section, be selective if it is a course or dish that you rarely make.

How many holiday events do I host per year? I host two dinners at Christmas (Christmas Eve and Christmas Day). I also host Easter and Thanksgiving and about two barbecues per year. At this writing, I am thirty-five years old. I expect to be cooking for at least another fifty years—so why would I need three hundred different holiday menus? Given that new menus are constantly featured in magazines and that paper disintegrates over the decades, I stick to about ten in my stockpile. Also consider whether you have a family tradition in place. This past Christmas, I made the most delectable prime rib and Yorkshire pudding that any of my twelve guests had ever tasted. By an overwhelming vote (including people who weren't there but heard about it), it has been determined that I shall make this annually. Therefore, saving a pile of "main holiday-fare feasts" is not necessary.

Activity One: Master Recipe Collection Qualifications
What qualifications will your recipes meet? List them on a sheet of paper, and then place this qualification list on the inside of your binder for quick reference.

Step Two: Cut and Categorize

Cut and Paste
Now that you have your criteria, browse through your cooking magazines. Look for recipes that meet the criteria created in Activity One. When you find one, cut it out and immediately paste or tape it to a sheet of paper so it doesn't get lost. Paste recipes of the same category on the same page. I only paste recipes on one side; this way if I want to reorder them for any reason, I can do so easily.

Create Your Categories
I recommend building your categories as needed versus creating them first. This ensures that you don't create categories you don't need. For example, if I only have twenty desserts, do I really need to separate them into cookies, brownies, cakes, pies, etc.?

Resist the temptation to over-organize. As soon as you over-organize a system, it loses its efficiency. The odds of maintaining it decrease drastically. If you create twenty subcategories for desserts and ten for side dishes and twenty for main dishes—imagine how many tabs you have to sort through to find the "correct" page to paste a recipe in the future. Keep it simple.

Caution: Don't assume the "Obvious Categories" are necessarily the best.

If I ask you to think of cooking categories, what categories come to mind? Most people will say desserts, soups and salads, breads, fish, beef, poultry, vegetarian, side dishes, and the like.

These categories might be the most natural fit for you, but before creating your tabs, consider how you approach cooking. Here are some factors to consider:

What is the average time you have to devote to cooking a recipe? If you find that you are constantly looking for quick-and-easy recipes, create a separate category for these main courses. You can even do quick-and-easy chicken, quick-and-easy beef, etc., if you find that you often need to search "on the fly" based on whatever main ingredient you have in house.

If you regularly plan ahead, I would avoid subdividing by entrée type (fish, vegetarian, etc.).

Create a separate category for "leisure recipes." During the week, our family focus is quick and easy. On weekends we usually go out one night and cook on the other. I keep a limited stock of leisure recipes in their own category. I don't let this category get too cumbersome, seeing as we only have one recipe per week from this category.

Do you create menu plans? If you plan menus a few days ahead or a week at a time, consider pasting all the components of the meal on one page. For example, in addition to your main course, add your side-dish recipe and vegetable recipe to the same page. This makes for quick shopping-list compilation. Worst case scenario, you can just grab however many nights you want to prep for, remove them from your binder, check off ingredients you have on hand, and take them to the store with you. Also, when it comes time to prepare your meal, all the recipes are on one page.

Do you cook for different people at different times? (If you cook primarily for yourself most of the time, you can skip this one.) Are there nights where you cook for yourself (or adults) separately than children? Or nights where you cook only for yourself? If so, consider the following category additions.

- **Kid Friendly:** These are recipes the kids like, but you would rather have something else. (If everyone would like it, it should stay with your general family recipes.)

- **Adults Only:** These are recipes your children refuse to eat.
- **Just for Me:** These are recipes only you like, for nights when you prepare your own meal.
- **Just for Others:** If you sometimes cook for other family members specifically, give them a category. (You do not need a category for each family member.) Simply write the individual's name at the top of the page.
- **Special Occasions:** What special occasions do you host throughout the year? Group those recipes in their own category so that you don't have to flip through them on a regular basis when planning day-to-day meals.
- **Entertaining:** If you entertain in addition to holidays, consider making a separate tab for these recipes.

Keeping these ideas and your own approach to cooking in mind, create your categories, and write them down on a separate sheet of paper as you go. Place this page in the front of your binder to help you quickly file recipes into the best section.

Cookbooks
I went through my cookbooks in the exact same manner I did my magazines, cutting out recipes based on the previous criteria. I was amazed to find only about 10 percent of the average cookbook interested me! I added them to my binder to create a "customized cookbook" that matched my needs. My neighbor was excited to take the cut-up cookbooks off my hands—her family has different tastes, and she found many recipes while helping me conquer my recipe clutter! I know it can be hard to cut up a book. I had an initial fear when I made my first incision. Yet my goal is not to read a cookbook but to use it. If I left it in full form, I would rarely cook the recipes my family liked, because I would forget they were there or not have time to fetch the cookbook prior to meal preparation.

Step Three: Maintain Your Collection

- **Track it!** Your collection is bound to include many recipes you have yet to try. Make sure to track what you like and what you don't! If you make a new recipe and no one likes it, place a big X over it. If you have the recipes sorted into menus and the side dish isn't a hit, put an X over it, and then look for a new one to paste right on top to try next time. It is very important to mark which recipes you like and which recipes you don't in order to keep the system functional.

- **Make room to grow.** Over time, your binder will grow! When filled to capacity, transfer the largest category into its own binder. For example, if you find you have mostly quick-and-easy recipes, move them into their own binder, and leave all other categories together. Add new binders only when you run out of space.

- **Add family favorites.** Transfer existing family recipes or recipe cards to your binder. Create a tab of "family approved" recipes. If you have compiled your recipes on recipe cards, you can either paste them in like any other printed page, or if they have writing on both sides, purchase clear photo pages and insert the recipes cards into the photo slots.

Take as long as you need to create your customized cookbook. Consider it a work in progress that will be added to for years to come — and likely a coveted heirloom!

Bonus Activity: For the Advanced Cooking Librarian

You can create your own binder index by numbering the pages by category. Do not number straight through, or you will not be able to add pages without numbering out of sequence — which defeats the purpose. For example, for the desserts category, I write D-1, D-2, D-3, etc. For the family dinner category, I write FD-1, FD-2, and so on.

Create a category index with page numbers, and place it at the front of each category, if you so desire. Whether or not you choose to go to this level of detail is up to your personal preference. I suggest starting without an index; then if you need one, you can always add it. This way you do not create a system more complex than you will want — or need — to maintain.

mini-makeover

mastering meal planning

"Cooking is like love. It should be entered into with abandon or not at all."—*Harriet Van Horne*

While it may seem menu planning is an insurmountable, time-consuming task, I have found that when you break it down into manageable steps, menu planning is actually a great time-saver. Here are some of the ways I <u>don't</u> spend my time with a menu plan in place:

- Listening to (or answering) the question, what's for dinner?
- Personally wondering what's for dinner
- Looking up the number for and calling a local delivery service
- Making extra trips to the grocery store
- Playing the game "What can I make with this?" as I stare at the few odd ingredients left in my kitchen—like a can of soup, container of breadcrumbs, and bag of flour

In this Mini you will learn how to realize the same benefits through the use of weekly meal plans.

Action Step Checklist

- ☐ Set up a recipe zone with the basic supply list.
- ☐ Begin gathering recipes and separating them into the designated categories.
- ☐ Check your calendar and your on-hand inventory before beginning your first weekly master menu.
- ☐ Create your master shopping list.
- ☐ Create your master weekly menu by following the steps listed in the Mini.

Early on in my meal-planning missions, I purchased several software programs, hoping each one would magically help my "undomestic" side and create a splendid dinner hour. The outcomes were far from stellar. First, the auto-generated lists contained many foods or recipes my family would not eat. Second, to create functional lists, I had to learn the software and enter all the information.

In addition to time-saving benefits, mastering meal planning also enables you to
- *reduce stress*
- *be in control of the portions (and avoid the supersized portions served in restaurants today)*
- *avoid impulse spending at the grocery store*
- *make cooking a family affair to encourage time together*
- *have a sit-down dinner and connect with others*
- *slow down and enjoy your meal versus inhaling it*
- *make food go further by planning well and cutting food waste*
- *improve nutrition by consuming fewer processed and convenience foods*

I finally found a software program I liked, only to discover the software had a bug—when I took my shopping list to the grocery store and saw one hundred pounds of onions on the list. While recipe software has advanced greatly and workable options do exist, I remain a firm believer that meal planning on paper is easiest—at least at first. Here's why: no matter what version of super-cooking software you purchase, the big question still has to be answered: what will you eat?

As you get used to the practice, you can build complicated menus and index your entire recipe collection into a computer program, if you like (I still do it by hand). But in the beginning, start small, focusing just on one week of dinner entrées at a time.

Gathering Recipes and Setting Up a Recipe Zone

You will need a small "recipe zone" for meal plan creation. When we finalize the meal plan, you will learn how to make a "master edition," which is simply a temporary holding area to keep your recipes and notes. Find your family description in the Creating Categories section to see how many categories you should create. Use a folder or envelope for each category.

Supply List
- Folders or envelopes (one for each category required by family size)
- Scissors
- Tape
- Recipes from websites, cookbooks, or recipe magazines (just a few—not the whole collection!)
- Pencil
- Grocery store flyer (if available for the week you are planning)
- Paper (preferably letter-sized and three-hole punched)

For later:
- Three-ring binder (half-inch or one-inch) to house your master lists and recipes
- Plastic sheet protectors to keep recipes safe from spills in the kitchen

Optional but handy:
- Tote bag, basket, or other container to store your supplies in and make this project portable

Create Your Categories

If you have both adults and children in your home, create four categories.
- **Everyone Likes:** These are recipes you have tried that all family members enjoyed.
- **Adults Only:** With taste buds varying so dramatically by age,

you may have quite a few recipes that Mom and Dad like but that leave the kids less than thrilled. Place those in this folder. (These recipes are great for when kids are at sleepovers.)

- **Kids Like; Adults Don't:** Likewise, you may have 10,800 pasta recipes for kids, but the adults in the household are on a protein diet. Place the recipes that are popular with kids but uninspiring to adults in this folder. (These are perfect recipes for you to use for weekend lunches or for a babysitter to prepare when you are out.)
- **Would Like to Try:** If you come across a cool recipe that sounds good but you haven't made it yet, place it in this folder.

If you have only adults in your household, you need only three categories:
- **Everyone Likes**
- **Some of Us Like**
- **Would Like to Try**

If you only prepare meals for yourself, you will need only two categories:
- **I Like**
- **I Would Like to Try**

Please complete this step before reading further.

Planning Your First Menu

While there are seven nights in a week, very few people will have a homemade dinner each of these nights. By thinking this through ahead of time, you avoid wasted food, time, and expense. I generally plan for five nights a week and keep a few super-quick solutions on standby in case of emergency. How many homemade meals will you eat, on average, per week?

Take a look at the Master Weekly Meal Plan worksheet. Notice the top row is blank instead of listing days of the week. This is because schedules so often change in this day and age, and we want the Master Weekly Meal Plan worksheet to work for **any week** so it can be recycled time and time again. To use the worksheet effectively, make sure to <u>only fill in</u> the number of days you indicated. For example, I cook five nights per week, so I would only fill in five columns. <u>Do not write in the days of the week at this time</u>.

Creating the Master Menu

- **Step One:** Consult your on-hand ingredients to see if there are any you would like to build your first menu around. Choose recipes from your recipe zone that everyone likes (or at least everyone will eat). Or combine recipes from the "kids like" and "adults like" categories to create a palatable dinner solution for all. Write these recipe ideas on the Main Dish row of the Master Weekly Meal Plan worksheet. If you do not have many ingredients on hand, consult the grocery-store flyer for current specials, and look for recipes that match the current special.
- **Step Two:** Add a fruit and/or vegetable to each meal in the row marked Fruits and/or Vegetables.
- **Step Three:** For meals where you will be serving a side dish, add a side dish in the applicable row.
- **Step Four:** The Other row is for any additional features of that particular meal such as a dessert.

Voila. You have created a weekly meal plan. This completed worksheet is your master copy. Make several photocopies, or type this into the computer so it can be reused. Tuck the master copy into a page protector in your three-ring binder. Behind it, add the recipes used. I paste the recipes to paper and then put the paper into page protectors.

After doing this for a while, you will have a good stock of weekly meal plans. When the weekly sale flyer comes from the grocery store, you can quickly grab a plan that matches the current special.

Creating the Master Shopping List

Gather all the recipes required for the meal plan. Work through the recipes one at a time, listing out necessary ingredients by category to make shopping easier. I do this in pencil so I can combine ingredients as I go. For example, I might need half of an onion in one recipe and then later find I need a whole onion for another recipe. By using pencil, I can change the quantity easily.

This shopping list is also a master copy. You do not want to rewrite it, so type it into the computer and print several copies, or make photocopies. Place these photocopies behind the Master Weekly Meal Plan worksheet in your recipe binder.

Suggested Shopping List Categories

Create your lists to coincide with the grocery store aisles to save time. Here are the categories I use:

- Produce
- Bread/Bakery
- Condiments
- Sauces/Spices
- Baking Supplies
- Packaged Meals/Soups
- Frozen Foods
- Meat
- Deli
- Milk/Dairy

Finalizing the Weekly Menu

Now that you have created a master copy of the Master Weekly Meal Plan worksheet, our last step is to customize a copy for the week you are planning.

- **Step One:** Look at your calendar. Are there any nights you will not be eating in? Write <u>only</u> the days that you will be eating in at the top of the meal plan.
- **Step Two:** If you know ahead of time that family members will not be attending, you might choose to add that to the notes row. If this involves several family members, consider adjusting the shopping list. If for some reason, plans have significantly altered, consider subbing a "would like to try" recipe. I use the Notes row for my husband, since his schedule is very unpredictable. Each week I have him write in what nights he will be gone.
- **Step Three:** In the "prep for tomorrow" column, look to see if there is anything you need to do ahead of time. For example, if you are having chicken on Tuesday but the chicken is frozen, you could write "transfer chicken to refrigerator" on Monday. Or if you are having a meal that requires diced onion tomorrow and you also need diced onion today, you might write "dice one cup onion," so you can do all the dicing in the same evening.
- **Step Four:** Post the meal plan on the refrigerator so everyone has the answer to the infamous question, what's for dinner?
- **Step Five:** Take a copy of the master shopping list and do a "walk-through," checking off any items you already have on hand.
- **Step Six:** Go shopping to pick up the remaining ingredients.
- **Step Seven:** Enjoy!

Menu Planning FAQ

What if we are all running every which way during the dinner hour? Set a time by choosing when the <u>most</u> family members can be present. Stick to this time every day. Let everyone know that <u>this</u> is when dinner is. As they make future arrangements, let them know that you expect them to work around the dinner hour. If they don't, that's okay. Don't cancel the dinner hour because someone can't attend. You owe it to yourself and other family members to prepare a healthy, quality meal — and more importantly, to sit down on a regular basis and enjoy a mealtime.

There is only me (or me and one other person). Should I cook a full meal every night? My husband travels three to five days per week, and we usually don't know until twenty-four hours beforehand when he will be gone. This makes meal planning very difficult. In the past, I often had dinner planned, and then if he would leave, I would just feed my daughter and not worry about my meal (or just make a snack). But then I realized that my daughter deserved the sit-down dinner hour. Now we have dinner together regularly — no matter what.

Tips for Cooking for One or Two

Before my husband and I had our daughter, it was just the two of us. Since he was often traveling, my dinner plans usually changed unexpectedly — should I prepare a meal for one or two? A few simple strategies helped me navigate the dinner hour.

- **Portion out one- or two-person servings and freeze the rest.** I found small disposable foil pans at the grocery store and began preparing items in individual servings. For example, I would cook a full lasagna but then store the leftovers in six or eight individual serving pans and freeze them. This created a very flexible system where I could grab one serving or two depending on the needs of the day.
- **Wash and prepare vegetables in advance; they will last longer.** Wash and slice unused portions of green and red peppers as well as onions. Place them on a tray or piece of freezer paper and place them flat in the freezer until frozen. After they have frozen, package them in freezer bags to use in cooked dishes.
- **Choose fresh vegetables that will keep well for a week or more.** Examples include beets, cabbage, carrots, celery, and squash. (Lettuce will generally keep about four days if washed and stored. You can also use a "salad keeper" to extend storage.)
- **Ask the butcher to cut any meat or fish into the size you need.**

- **Plan around perishables.** To minimize trips to the grocery store, plan meals with fresh fruits and vegetables on the night of the day you do your shopping (and/or the next day).
- **Experiment with microwave and slow-cooker recipes.** These can greatly simplify cooking. You can find sixteen sample microwave recipes specifically designed for cooking for one at www.microwavecookingforone.com/Content.html.
- **Lengthen the life of meat and poultry by freezing immediately.** As soon as you arrive home from the store, wrap individual servings of meat and poultry in freezer paper or food-storage-grade bags or containers and freeze. Make sure to date and label them to avoid the "mystery meat" game. Dating the item will help you know how long it can be saved. The following pages contain the Food and Drug Administration's storage guidelines.

Master Weekly Meal Plan Worksheet

Master Weekly Meal Plan						
Day of the Week						Prep Work
Main Dish						
Vegetable or Fruit						
Side Dish						
Other						
Notes						

Visit www.maketodaymatter.net for a full-size printable page.

Food Storage Guidelines

Raw Hamburger, Ground & Stew Meat	Refrigerator	Freezer
Hamburger & stew meats	1 to 2 days	3 to 4 months
Ground turkey, veal, pork, lamb	1 to 2 days	3 to 4 months

Ham, Corned Beef	Refrigerator	Freezer
Corned beef in pouch with pickling juices	5 to 7 days	Drained, 1 month
Ham, canned, labeled "Keep Refrigerated," unopened	6 to 9 months	Don't freeze
Ham, canned, labeled "Keep Refrigerated," opened	3 to 5 days	1 to 2 months
Ham, fully cooked, whole	7 days	1 to 2 months
Ham, fully cooked, half	3 to 5 days	1 to 2 months
Ham, fully cooked, slices	3 to 4 days	1 to 2 months

Hot Dogs & Lunch Meats	Refrigerator	Freezer (in freezer wrap)
Hot dogs, opened package	1 week	1 to 2 months
Hot dogs, unopened package	2 weeks	1 to 2 months
Lunch meats, opened package	3 to 5 days	1 to 2 months
Lunch meats, unopened package	2 weeks	1 to 2 months

Soups & Stews	Refrigerator	Freezer
Vegetable or meat-added & mixtures of them	3 to 4 days	2 to 3 months

Bacon & Sausage	Refrigerator	Freezer
Bacon	7 days	1 month
Sausage, raw from pork, beef, chicken, or turkey	1 to 2 days	1 to 2 months
Smoked breakfast links, patties	7 days	1 to 2 months
Summer sausage labeled "Keep Refrigerated," unopened	3 months	1 to 2 months
Summer sausage labeled "Keep Refrigerated," opened	3 weeks	1 to 2 months

Fresh Meat (Beef, Veal, Lamb & Pork)	Refrigerator	Freezer
Steaks	3 to 5 days	6 to 12 months
Chops	3 to 5 days	4 to 6 months
Roasts	3 to 5 days	4 to 12 months
Variety meats (tongue, kidneys, liver, heart, chitterlings)	1 to 2 days	3 to 4 months

Meat Leftovers	Refrigerator	Freezer
Cooked meat & meat dishes	3 to 4 days	2 to 3 months
Gravy & meat broth	1 to 2 days	2 to 3 months

Fresh Poultry	Refrigerator	Freezer
Chicken or turkey, whole	1 to 2 days	1 year
Chicken or turkey, parts	1 to 2 days	9 months
Giblets	1 to 2 days	3 to 4 months

Cooked Poultry, Leftover	Refrigerator	Freezer
Fried chicken	3 to 4 days	4 months
Cooked poultry dishes	3 to 4 days	4 to 6 months
Pieces, plain	3 to 4 days	4 months
Pieces covered with broth, gravy	1 to 2 days	6 months
Chicken nuggets, patties	1 to 2 days	1 to 3 months

Fish & Shellfish	Refrigerator	Freezer
Lean fish	1 to 2 days	6 months
Fatty fish	1 to 2 days	2 to 3 months
Cooked fish	3 to 4 days	4 to 6 months
Smoked fish	14 days	2 months
Fresh shrimp, scallops, crawfish, squid	1 to 2 days	3 to 6 months
Canned seafood, open, out of can	3 to 4 days	2 months
Canned seafood, unopened, 5 years		

Menu Tips

When creating your first meal plan, keep these tips in mind:

- **Take a quick visual check of your current food inventory.** *See if you have any main ingredients to work with. Write these down. As you build your first plan, look for recipes that maximize on-hand ingredients.*
- **Check the current grocery-store flyer for the weekly sales and specials.** *Most grocery stores operate on a three-week cycle. As you learn this cycle from planning, you will learn what to buy when. Try using the same "main ingredient" to minimize costs and spoilage. For example, you might want to feature beef one week and chicken another.*

  When I say this, I often hear, "What?? Eat beef all week?" I do not mean this literally. In the American meat-and-potatoes society, I have noticed the tendency for many meal planners to put meat as the star of every meal. Try featuring at least one meatless night per week, or at least let meat be the "supporting star" instead of the "show stopper." For my menu plans, I feature one meat per week (two to three nights) to reduce spoilage and maximize my grocery budget. The other nights are meatless recipes such as homemade pizza, lasagna, fettuccini, vegetable-and-rice stir fry, soup and salad, build-your-own baked potato bar, breakfast for dinner, etc.
- **Avoid including recipes from the "would like to try" category.** *Creating a weekly meal plan requires compiling a shopping list, so we want to make sure all the recipes are "keepers." I like to do my regular meal plans during the week and then on weekends experiment with new recipes. These come from the "would like to try" recipes. From these recipes, I add the ones that receive a "thumbs up" to the "everyone likes" category.*

mini-makeover

controlling your cosmetics

"I live by a man's code, designed to fit a man's world, yet at the same time I never forget that a woman's first job is to choose the right shade of lipstick."—*Carole Lombard*

Many women are drawn to cosmetics like a magnet. Before we know it, we are buried in every possible color, brand, shade, and option. Good makeup and skin care can make us feel wonderful. The wrong makeup and skin care can have the exact opposite effect. In this Mini we want to work to scale back our stock to focus in on the products that make us feel good and are still effective and safe.

Action Step Checklist
- ☐ Complete Step One.
- ☐ Complete Step Two.
- ☐ Complete Step Three by working through each of the 10 areas listed and utilizing the checklist in this Mini.
- ☐ Complete Step Four
- ☐ Complete Step Five

If you are among the ten percent of women that are not serial cosmetic purchasers, you likely did not choose this Mini. However, if you own more than ten lipsticks, you are in the right place. (Or if you own more than three eyeshadow compacts and one has blue eyeshadow, or is ten years old or older.)

As a fellow makeup-a-holic, I can honestly say I have tried just about every brand. I have bought-in to the "lose your crow's feet in three days" and other promises of expensive skin care. I have now trimmed back my makeup and skin care routine to my "tried and true" products. They are effective, complimentary, and yield a simple routine.

Our first mission is to prune through the existing piles. When we are done we will look at how to make "quick fix" bags for specific needs: day wear, evening wear (dramatic), skin care routine, pampering routine.

Step One: Glamour Gathering
Begin by collecting all of your makeup and skin care in **one** central location (this includes the stuff in the back of the closet, in the bottom drawer, in various purses, in the compartment in the car, etc.).

Step Two: Group Like Items Together
Use plastic storage bags, paper bags, or miscellaneous boxes and bins to group like items together. Put all lipsticks in one container, all eyeshadows in another, all lip pencils in yet another. Place all cleanser together, all toner together, mascara, etc.

Step Three: The First Pass
We are going to work through each group one at a time. Our first pass is devoted to getting rid of anything outdated. It would be hard to do this in a day!

Instead, spread it out by working on one to two "categories" from the checklist daily. (The checklist is at the end of Step Three.) Try to work through all of the categories this week for the "toss" step.

> **Tip from the FDA**
> *You may also need to watch certain "all natural" products that contain substances taken from plants. These products may be more at risk for bacteria. Since these products contain no preservatives or have nontraditional ones, your risk of infection may be greater. If you don't store these products as directed, they may expire before the expiration date.*

- **Mascaras:** Experts agree that three months is the maximum safe time for mascara. If you can't stomach three months, then keep for six months. Anything over that should be discarded as it is a breeding ground for bacteria.
- **Blush:** Using these guidelines, work through your blushes and discard anything that could be contaminated or ineffective.
- **Eyeshadows:** Again using the cream and powder guidelines, work through your collection discarding anything that could be contaminated or ineffective.
- **Lipstick:** Experts recommend tossing lipstick and lip gloss after two years as it will dry out. The water content within the lipstick can help to breed bacteria. Long-wearing formulas often have a shorter life span.
- **Liners (lip and eye):** Liners generally last three years, provided they are sharpened regularly. If you have not used a liner in a while, make sure to sharpen well to reveal all "fresh" cosmetic before use. Liquid liners should be treated like mascara and tossed after three months.
- **Foundation (and concealer):** The experts weigh in at six months for liquid foundation and two years for powder foundation. One hundred percent pure mineral makeup such as Bare Essentuals is often said to never expire. While the minerals would last indefinitely, remember that exposure to air is what can cause bacteria to gather on the container. It is likely safe for three years.
- **Skin Care Products:** Skin care products that are FDA regulated usually have an expiration date. Begin by checking these and discarding anything that has expired.

Cosmeceuticals (products claiming to have anti-aging and skin-changing benefits) are not regulated, and once they've been used, they should be tossed between six months and a year. A lot depends on the ingredients—some actually become more potent over time such as retinol and glycolic acid, and can cause unwanted effects. If in doubt, look up the active ingredient online.

- **Nail Polish:** One to two years
- **Hair Products:** One year

Cosmetic Control Action Checklist

	Mascara	Blush	Lipstick	Foundation & Concealer	Hair Products
Toss					
Try					

	Lip Liner	Nail Polish	Eyeliner	Eyeshadow
Toss				
Try				

Checklist
Work through each of your makeup collections with these guidelines. Place a checkmark in the "toss" box when you have completed each collection. The "try" row will be our next activity.

Step Four: Try It On
Again, doing all of the following steps in a day would be difficult and likely leave you with sore skin! Instead work through the areas at a one a day pace.

1. Sit down near your makeup with a mirror and a mug of coffee or tea.

2. Start with lipsticks and a good bottle of makeup remover. Try each one on. If it is dry, throw it out. If it makes you look like a clown, throw it out.

3. Move on to foundations and powders. If they do not blend into your skin seamlessly, throw them out. If they are cakey, throw them out.

4. Repeat this process with each product on the action checklist, throwing out any colors that make you look or feel clown-like. Obviously you won't get to do this all in a day—break it up into components. As you complete each makeup type, place a checkmark in the "try" column of the action checklist.

5. Analyze all your skin care products. If it doesn't work, throw it out.

6. You do not need to try nail polish on; just paint a bit on a sheet of paper to make sure it is still good and a color you would wear.

7. Mascara also does not need to be tried as long as you have followed the toss guidelines. You may want to check the wands, though, to make sure the mascara is not dry or lumpy. You can easily clean the wand with a piece of tissue to remove any lumps.

8. If you have hair products you have not yet tried, set them out and then use different products each day to check their effectiveness.

(**Important note:** if you can't bring yourself to throw out these often expensive items, at least put them in a bag so we can get them out of the way for now.)

Once this is complete we will talk about organizing your items into "ideal looks" and a system for keeping cosmetics under control. But first, let's get to work on these steps.

Step Five: Create Your Look

Now that we have everything "pruned" it is time to get to work with a strategy that will keep us organized and looking our best.

You will need small zipper cosmetic bags. If you don't have any lying around, zipper-top plastic bags will work just fine.

The Basic Bag
The basic bag should contain the cosmetic items you use every day no matter what (or the days you wear makeup anyway). These are the items that do not change day to day. For example, my basic bag has:
- Foundation primer
- Foundation
- A cosmetic sponge
- Loose powder
- Loose powder brush
- Concealer
- Brow pencil
- Eyelash curler
- Mascara
- Eyeshadow brushes
- Blush brush
- Concealer brush

The next time you do your makeup, put all your non-changing basics into one bag.

The Five-Minute Face Bag
The Five-Minute Face bag is for a simple makeup look of colors you love and can apply quickly for a simple makeup routine. My "Five-Minute Face" bag has:
- Eyeliner
- Blush
- Two eye brushes
- Lip stain
- Lip gloss

If you like to alter your looks and wear warm colors on some days and cool colors on others, create two or more bags. For example, your brown and natural colors could go in one, pinks in another. The key to a successful Five-Minute Face bag is to focus on basic looks and colors that work with almost anything for everyday wear.

The Diva Bag
The Diva bag is for a more dramatic look worn for evening, formal occasions, or whenever you feel the call to go dramatic. The best way to create the Diva bag is to try on your makeup and find a dramatic look you love and then collect the items in one location.

Create as many looks as you desire. Store your dramatic looks together in a drawer or closet shelf. Leave your basic bag and Five-Minute Face bags in your most accessible areas.

Skin Care
The simplest solution I have found for skin care is a caddy with two openings and handle in the middle (like those used to store cleaning supplies.) On the left I put all of my morning routine items; on the right I put my evening routine items. Using bags or a caddy, collect your routine in one spot. Remember to use your oldest products up first to avoid spoilage.

Putting Everything in Its Place
I store this under the sink to keep the counter clear and I store my frequently used looks in my vanity drawer. I keep all the "leftovers" together, bagged by type in a basket. Then when I feel the urge for a "new look," I go "shopping" in my basket versus at the store.

mini-makeover

beautifying your home

"Learn how to be happy with what you have while you pursue all that you want."—*Jim Rohn*

Taking steps to create a dream home for you and your family does not require a multi-thousand dollar budget or a designer's help. You can approach your home simply—one day and one step at a time. In fact, that is exactly what we will do in this Mini.

Action Step Checklist
- ☐ Read Step One.
- ☐ Complete the Room worksheets for each room of your home.
- ☐ Read and complete the Tips for Discovering Your Personal Style.
- ☐ Read the Exploring Color section.
- ☐ Explore the color resources.
- ☐ Read the information on idea gathering.
- ☐ Choose one room to focus on first and begin gathering ideas.
- ☐ Read the Building an Action Plan and the Master Room worksheet instructions.
- ☐ Complete the first page of the Master Room worksheet for your chosen room.
- ☐ Complete the second page of the Master Room worksheet for your chosen room.
- ☐ Review the tips at the end of the Mini.
- ☐ Take action...and enjoy!

As a frequent traveler, I'm often amazed at how dramatically my mood changes depending on where I am staying. I have stayed in some very nice hotels; so warm and welcoming I loved being in my room. Other rooms were so dark and uninviting I found my mood spiraling downward. Our environment and surroundings play a huge part in how we feel on a day-to-day basis. Think about it: When your home is messy, chaotic, cluttered, and filled with piles, how do you feel? My guess is "stressed" is among the adjectives that top your list. Likewise, when our homes are clean and straightened we feel more at peace.

Ideally our homes should be a place where function meets personal fashion, creating a sanctuary to rest, rejuvenate, roam, and recharge.

The task of beautifying your home will be an ongoing process. I recommend keeping a completely separate binder for this project. Sheet protectors or slash pockets will also be helpful to hold clippings, pictures, and ideas. You may also want to add a zipper pouch with scissors and a glue stick so you always have your "beautify supplies" at the ready when you want to work on your book.

This Mini is divided into four sections:

Step One: Evaluate

Step Two: Explore and Collect Color

Step Three: Idea Gathering

Step Four: Create an Action Plan

Step One: Evaluate

The process of going through your home to add more style, function, and beauty is much like the process we use in the Extreme Home Makeover course or when building routines in the Toolbox—a walk-through is in order. Choose a room in which to start. Sit down for a good twenty minutes, really taking in all the items, furniture, textures, and colors of the room.

During this time complete the Room worksheet. Do not worry if you do not have all the answers now; simply write down what you do know at this point. I encourage you to complete a Room worksheet for each room in your home before moving onto Step Two. At minimum answer the first two questions on Part One of the Room worksheet and the first two on Part Two of the Room worksheet.

These answers will help when making decisions about what to move, simplify, and change when we get to the Action Plan.

Room Worksheet
Part One

Room Name _____

Room Function (Activities)

_____

_____

_____

_____

How often is this room used?

_____

_____

_____

_____

Is there a focal point or "main attraction" to the room that you like? (Examples: a painting, an arrangement, etc.)

_____

_____

_____

_____

When people are in this room, what mood would you like to be reflected? (Examples: Focus, relaxation, excitement, calm, playfulness)

_____

_____

What are the predominant colors?

_____

_____

_____

Room Worksheet: Part Two

What in the room does not serve the activities listed on the room worksheet? Where can it be moved?

_____

_____

_____

_____

Is there anything that should be in this room to use in activities? What? Where would it go?

_____

_____

_____

_____

Tip: *One of the main reasons a house ends up in disarray is that items are not stored near where they are most often used. By keeping items near their point of use, odds are much better that they will make it back home versus becoming unnecessary clutter.*

What will remain (or what would you like to make) the focal point of the room? If you aren't sure then just make a note that you need one—and keep this in mind during the idea gathering process.

_____

_____

_____

_____

Colors (See the additional tips on Choosing Colors in this Mini.) Based on the mood you would like to elicit in this room, what colors would you like to explore?

_____

_____

_____

Style-Discovery: Tips for Finding Your Style
The well-decorated home has a style that unites each of the rooms
into a welcoming whole. The style can be subtle or bold, but it's
there. How do you uncover your personal style? You start by doing
a little detective work in your interests. This detective work pays
off by helping you to avoid impulse decisions or purchases. When
adding or removing decorations you can ask: **Does this item reflect
my style?**

Existing Style: Does a color or a specific style seem to emerge
repeatedly throughout your home? Look to see what you have
collected in your rooms, as hidden underneath are often a few clues
to your personal style.

On the Wall: What types of pictures or art have you chosen for
your walls? What themes, colors, emotions, and styles emerge?

_____

_____

_____

_____

Better with Age? When you furniture shop, do you look for antiques
or handed down items or are you off to find something new?

_____

_____

Impulse: Find three or four household items you recently purchased
on impulse such as a picture frame, placemat, bedspread, knickknack,
towel, or soap dish. What do they have in common? Color? Style?

_____

_____

_____

What are three words you can use to describe your personal style
based on your observations?

_____

_____

Step Two: Explore and Collect Color

Color is one of the simplest tools for decorating—once you understand how it affects the overall mood of the room and how to use it. The articles and resources in this section will help you choose colors to create the atmosphere you desire. Remember—choosing a color doesn't mean you need to repaint the room! You can add color through throw pillows, blinds, decorations, art, painting trim, and many other ways!

Many paint companies, such as Behr, offer free comprehensive online tools to help you explore color. At www.behr.com you can explore color theory and create a free online workbook to store your findings.

Next, take the predominant colors of the room you are working with and find a close match in the color center. This will help you see the existing mood you are creating and suggest effective complimentary colors for your decorating. (Make sure to print a copy to add to your book.)

Another neat way to interact with the site is to look at rooms in different colors. Note what mood and atmosphere the color gives off. You can do this using the color menu. Follow the INSPIRATION link and then choose "Our Galleries" and finally "Color."

Other Cool Sites to Browse: These sites contain additional reading and tips for using color to maximize your home's beauty.
www.hgtv.com/topics/interior-paint-colors/index.html
www.myhomeideas.com/myhome?
www.colorstrology.com

Tip: *The interior design rule of thumb is to use three colors in a room and a 60-30-10 theory. Sixty percent should be the predominant color, thirty percent your second accent color, and ten percent your third accent color.*

Step Three: Idea-Gathering

Gathering ideas can be a very fun step. Begin by paging through magazines and finding attractive rooms. For example, if you are working on your living room, begin by finding living rooms that have a theme or feel you would like to emulate in your own home. Don't worry if you can't find something that is exactly like what you want; you can clip furniture from one picture and paintings from another. Here are a few more sources for idea-gathering:

1. **If you have a friend** who has a "knack" for displays and interior design, consider seeking her help and recommendations. Make sure to share what you have discovered and recorded thus far in your Beauty Book.

2. **Visit furniture stores,** antique shops, and department stores to gather ideas for displays and decoration. Check your local library and bookstore for additional books and ideas.

3. **Better Homes and Gardens** offers a great gallery of over 18,000 rooms divided by category. This is a great way to browse rooms to find things you like! Check it out at: www.bhg.com/premium/decorate/?psrc= didecchannel.

4. **Visit your local improvement store.** Look at their idea books and magazines. Find paint samples and color palettes that are appealing to you.

5. **Think simple:** Often an arrangement or focal point can be a quick fix using items you have on hand. Watch for simple arrangements of objects, pictures, knickknacks, and the like that appeal to you. Use these as templates to create a similar grouping. (This is typically where I start as it maximizes what I have on hand.)

6. **Simplest Design Trick:** Often removing items can be the quickest way to unify a design. Look for items that do not match the colors or mood you wish to create. Rearrange items you do have into attractive arrangements, creating points of interest in the room. You can test for points of interest by walking into a room and seeing what first catches your eye. If you eye is wandering without a "stopping point," then think about how to develop stronger points of interest.

7. **Screen-Shop:** Instead of window shopping, screen shop. One of my favorite sites (and reasonably priced as well) is www.homedecorators.com. You can use this to find items

or ideas and with a wide selection of styles and products it makes it a great place to collect images and clips for your home Beauty Book.

Let the process of gathering ideas take as long as you desire. Remember that this is a work in progress. The collecting is half the fun! Once you have some ideas, pick one to start. I encourage you to work through one room at a time, completing it in its entirety before moving to the next room. This way you will be able to enjoy one room while working on the others and not cause a lot of clutter or disruption in the home.

Remember that decorating and performing a facelift to a room needn't be costly or time consuming. Adding a new print to a wall, colorful pillows to a couch, or a few plants can breathe new life into a tired room.

Step Four: Building the Action Plan

As you begin to collect ideas, you will likely find that one room seems to take "shape" more than the others. Perhaps you have the right additions, arrangements, or colors. When you reach that point you want to make sure to record your observations on a final room worksheet. Place the final room worksheet in a sheet protector and then place any related clipped images, color swatches, etc., behind it. I also recommend pasting a copy of your predominant colors onto the page itself in the Color Swatch area. This can be very handy should you need to shop for an item.

List out any items you would like to purchase, along with the price and vendor information. (Think of this as a "wish list"; you aren't expected to go shopping today!) Having a list of items helps you to focus on what you want—and you may find less expensive alternatives. For example I was shocked at the price to remodel my whole kitchen—but I found just updating the knobs on the doors with color gave it a fresh new look. (We have lots of cabinet and drawer knobs!) In addition, list out any action steps you need to take such as moving items to another room.

Instructions for Master Room Worksheet

Write the room and the mood you are aiming to convey at the top of the sheet.

In the Color Swatches boxes, paste in samples of your chosen colors. In the area for name/color code, write the actual color name (either from the Pantone site or paint chip). You may also want to record the actual CMYK code. This ensures the color can be duplicated consistently.

On the Wish List, write down any items you see that fit your designing goals.

On the Action Steps Checklist, record tasks that need to be completed. (Check your Room worksheets for ideas on what needs to be moved, simplified, and the like. Make sure to list individual action steps, adding pages as needed, instead of projects.) Use the resources column to list items where you need to hire someone or, if you have someone you can delegate to, write his or her name.

Master Room Worksheet

Room Name _____

Mood:

Color Swatches (See the designer tip on page 116):

Main Color	Secondary Color	Third/Accent Color
Color Name/Code		

Wish List

Item/Description	Store	SKU/Item #	Price

Action Steps Checklist

Task	Resources	Start Date (goal)	Finish Date (goal)	Complete

Simple Ideas to Give a Room a Facelift

- **Color:** Do the walls represent the room? If your house has all white walls, consider toying with color. Painting a room is the quickest way to give it a fresh look. Stenciling is another option for those who don't want to brave a full paint makeover. If you want to keep your white walls, are there prints or paintings that could be added to give the room a new tone? What types of prints and paintings would you enjoy—abstract, contemporary, wildlife? What colors should the paintings emphasize to help coordinate the overall color of the room? (See the additional tips on choosing colors in this Mini.)

- **Furniture:** Are there pieces of furniture that need to be refinished, repaired, or replaced? Are there any pieces you would like to add?

- **Windows:** Do you like your current window coverings? If not, what would you prefer? Would you like to go with a valance? Blinds? No coverings?

- **Decorations:** What elements could be added to change the tone of the room? How about a small water fountain in a room where you like to relax? Fountains can be found very inexpensively at stores like Target or Wal-Mart. Would an arrangement of candles or dried flowers add to the room? Could you remove items to simplify the space? Could you swap items with items from another area of the house for a fresh feel?

- **Foliage:** What about plants? Plants quickly provide a new feel within a room. If you have a bad history with plants, don't despair. Visit your local garden center and explain you want a very durable plant for someone without a "green thumb." These garden experts can help you pick the plant that is best for you.

- **Floor covering:** How do you want your floors to look? Would you like rugs, floor coverings, hardwood, or to lay new tile?

mini-makeover

responsibilities and rewards

"Man is always more than he can know of himself; consequently, his accomplishments, time and again, will come as a surprise to him."—*Golo Mann*

Chore and reward systems are incredibly effective and beneficial with children. A good system can inspire children while teaching them responsibility and discipline. It also allows you to delegate some tasks to children and remove them from your personal to-do list. I have found these systems are more effective than allowances, since they visually show children how to choose a goal and work toward it. In this Mini I'll share a successful and versatile reward and responsibility program.

Action Step Checklist
- ☐ Complete Step One.
- ☐ Complete Step Two.
- ☐ Complete Step Three.
- ☐ Complete Step Four.
- ☐ Put the system into action!
- ☐ Refresh monthly.

My latest chore and reward rendition was inspired after having two high-school age kids work for me over the course of a summer. Each day their tasks varied greatly. Sometimes they would help assemble products, sometimes they worked in the yard, other times they would move or organize items in my home. At first I tried giving them a list to work from but often if the list was not incredibly detailed they would forget the exact task. Since I didn't have a lot of time to write a list, I asked my assistant, Mike, to take over. I would give my assistant a list of what I needed done and then he would walk the two teens through it. Within a few days the two teens were completing many more tasks—and more thoroughly. I decided to watch my assistant one morning to see what he was doing that worked so well.

Mike had the list I gave him on a clipboard along with a pad of Post-It notes. He would walk through the area and explain the task and then put a Post-It note with a few keywords on the item(s) related to the task. For example if a bunch of stuff needed to be moved from the second floor to the basement, he would put a sticky on each piece that required moving with the word "move." If CDs needed to be put back in their containers, in the CD area he would write "put back in case" and place the sticky on the CD shelf. Over the course of this walk-through with the two kids Mike might make fifty Post-It notes. He kept track of how many he made on his clipboard. Then the teens would "get to work" and retrieve each Post-It note as they completed the task, turning in the finished pile at the end of the day so Mike could see exactly what was accomplished.

This system seemed to work in several ways:
- It provided an easy visual so the teens could maximize their time, completing all like tasks in a given room before moving onto another.
- The teens felt a greater sense of accomplishment building this pile of Post-Its than they did with a checklist.

The concept reminded me of an Easter Egg hunt in a work environment. Hunt for the eggs (which were tasks in this case) and reap the reward (which was pay in this case).

Seeing how this system was so much more effective than the typical checklist chart, I began brainstorming a way to transform this into a system of cooperation and teamwork to complete household chores and maintenance. Within a few months I had my Chore Responsibility Rewards program up and running.

Tip: Read this entire Mini through once and then read a second time, completing the activities during the second reading.

Here is the premise:

Cards are created to align with tasks that need to be completed around the home. These cards each have a point value based on the time involved and the difficulty. (Points can vary by age group if you have children spanning a range of ages.) One side of the card serves as an instruction guide, the other is a date tracker—much like a library card.

The cards are displayed in pockets in a high-visible area (like the front of the refrigerator) or in a photo-book on an easel. A person visits the cards to see what needs to be completed, chooses his or her task(s) and when done, he or she dates and initials the back of the card. The card is then returned to a "completed" pocket. After checking the work (if necessary) you then award points, which are tracked on a register and then redeemed.

Points can be redeemed for anything you desire—from simple privileges like choosing what's for dinner, or choosing the restaurant or movie next time your family goes out, or for allowance. Alternatively, you can also use a quota system that requires each family member to perform "X" points as part of their contribution to the family.

Choosing a Goal. Before you can begin to design the system you need to choose a goal that is largely dependent on your parenting style. Some parents believe that all tasks should be done as part of the contribution to the family unit. Other parents believe all tasks should be rewarded and still other parents fall somewhere in-between. Knowing your position on rewards for responsibility is important because it allows you to choose tasks consistent with the goal.

Let me share my viewpoint, not to influence your own but to give you an idea of how you would choose the goal. I fall somewhere in the middle category, believing that basic tasks should be completed as part of the family unit. Outside of basic tasks, if my daughter is going to spend time working around the home instead of playing, reading, or being with friends, I believe in rewarding her contribution.

With this philosophy in mind, I would create a contribution quota to reflect what I feel is the basis of contributing within the family. Each week she would need to reach this point quota at a minimum, and then anything in excess of this quota would be points that could be redeemed. For example, if she were to complete thirty points worth of tasks and the quota was set at ten points, she would have twenty points in rewards. (You do not need to know the quota right now, just whether or not you will offer rewards.)

If you are not going to offer rewards then consider recording only the routine expected tasks, but avoid more difficult tasks. You can also use a plus and minus system where behavior and tasks are rewarded but undesirable behavior results in points being subtracted. Choose whatever technique aligns with your parenting style. If you are unsure, complete the reading of this entire Mini first so you have an idea of how the system works.

Will your system offer:
____ *Rewards only?*
____ *Responsibilities only?*
____ *Responsibilities and rewards?*
____ *Rewards, responsibilities, and repercussions?*

Creating the System

Step One: Delegation Factor

First, it is important to make sure the tasks you pick are able to be delegated. When delegating, you cannot expect perfection. We will work through how to get the best results possible a bit later. Generally, I like to use this rule of thumb: **If this task was completed at least 75 percent as well as I am capable of, would that be satisfactory?** If the answer is yes, then I consider the task to be a good delegate candidate. If my answer is no, then that is a task best reserved for me. Your threshold may be higher or lower, but choose one that works for you and make sure the tasks you collect in the next step meet that threshold.

Tip: *Avoid micromanaging when delegating tasks or criticizing if someone has done their best work. Be open to the fact they may complete the task differently and that is okay as long as it reaches the 75 percent quota.*

Step Two: Task Collecting

Next you will need to gather the following information about the tasks in your home and add it to the Task List worksheet on page 137. (Do not worry about the last three columns yet.)

- **Task:** List a few words to remind you of the task you are going to write on the card. Remember to be specific for example "sweep kitchen" is specific; "clean kitchen" is not.
- **Frequency:** How often does this task need to be completed? Daily? Weekly? Monthly? Quarterly? Is this a one-time or as-needed task?
- **Time needed:** How much time does this task take? Feel free to give a range. Also err on the side of caution, remembering that if people have not done this task before, they may not be as fast as you! Write the time down in minutes. Sometimes the time required and difficulty vary with age. For example, it will take a five-year-old longer to sweep than a teen

(and be more challenging). If you are working with kids separated by several years or more, make a worksheet for each age group. List the task on each worksheet and then assess the time separately (as well as the difficulty) for each age group.

- **Difficulty:** Is this a mucky task like cleaning the toilet? Will it involve getting dirty? Is it physically demanding like yard work or lifting? Circle one for easy, two for medium, and three for difficult. Again, keep in mind this might vary with age.
- **Age limit:** Is this task only appropriate for specific ages in your home? If so, list the age-appropriate range, example thirteen and up. If you have a separate worksheet by age group, then this step is not required since only the age-appropriate tasks need to be written down.

Break it down: The system works most effectively with tasks requiring less time. If you have tasks requiring over an hour of work try breaking them down into thirty-minute increments. The younger the participants, the shorter time span the tasks need to be.

Complete at least one page of tasks before moving onto the next step. Consult your master Task List worksheet for ideas or walk through your home looking for areas where you could use a helping hand.

Step Three: Determining Task Values

I have created the following chart as a guideline for assigning point values. I have also included a blank chart should you wish to create your own.

To determine a point value for a task, first check your Task List worksheet to see how long the task takes. Find that number in the Minutes column and then look across the table to the base points. Write this in the top quarter of the Point Equation column of your Task List Worksheet. Next, look at the difficulty you recorded on the Task List Worksheet. Find the difficulty in the top row and then follow it down to where it intersects the time required. Record any additional points you find in this box on the bottom quarter of the cell. Add the two numbers together to get the point value total.

Example

Task: Mopping the kitchen floor
Time required: Fifteen minutes
Difficulty: Medium

In the first column I find the number: fifteen minutes. I then go to the next column, "Base Points," and see this is a "3." I write that down in the Points Equation box. Then I find the Difficulty in the same row. There are not any bonus points awarded for a fifteen-minute task of medium difficulty so I would write down zero in the other part of the point equation box. Obviously 3 + 0 = 3, which is what would go in the Point Value column of the Task List Worksheet. While you could do the math in your head, should you need to alter or tweak the system down the road, having it broken out is often helpful.

Point Value Reference Guide

Minutes	Base Points	Easy (1)	Medium (2)	Hard (3)
5	1	0	0	0
10	2	0	0	0
15	3	0	0	½
20	4	0	0	½
25	5	0	0	1
30	6	0	½	1
35	7	0	½	1
40	8	0	½	1 ½
45	9	0	½	1 ½
50	10	0	½	1 ½
55	11	0	½	2
60	12	0	1	2
65	13	0	1	2

Continued...

Minutes	Base Points	Easy (1)	Medium (2)	Hard (3)
70	15	0	1	2 ½
75	16	0	1	2 ½
80	18	0	1 ½	2 ½
85	19	0	1 ½	3
90	20	0	1 ½	3

Note: in my chart you'll notice the points earned per period increase slightly when a task is seventy minutes or more. This is to encourage completion of some of the longer tasks that otherwise may not get done. I personally do not create any tasks more than ninety minutes in length. Generally I try to keep tasks to thirty minutes where possible.

Point Value Reference Guide

Minutes	Base Points	Easy	Medium	Hard
5				
10				
15				
20				
25				
30				
35				
40				
45				
50				
55				
60				
65				
70				
75				
80				
85				
90				

Tip: When possible, make tasks sixty minutes or less. Generally speaking, people are motivated by the more they get done, therefore you will likely see better results with several smaller tasks than one large task.

Step Four: Creating Your Cards

With the tasks recorded, it is time to create the cards that will be used in the system. You will find templates with this Mini. Note that the cards are color-coded, offering six different colors. I use the colors to denote frequency (optional):

- Daily
- Weekly
- Monthly
- Quarterly
- Yearly
- As-Needed

Sample Card

Instructions
✓ If the dishwasher has clean dishes inside, put all of the dishes away into their proper places. ✓ Rinse dirty dishes in the sink, using a sponge if necessary, and then place them in the dishwasher. Plates and larger dishes go on the bottom rack, cups, mugs, and bowls on the top rack. ✓ Place utensils in the tableware compartment, placing some with the eating side pointed up and others pointed down. One exception: knives should always be pointed down. ✓ Leave a little space between the dishes—you do not want them to touch or they might break. ✓ When full, take one of the dishwasher packets beneath the sink and place in the open compartment on the backside of the dishwasher door. (You can see this when the dishwasher is open.) ✓ Push the button that says "Accusense." ✓ Push the Start button. ✓ Make sure you hear the dishwasher start before walking away (or you may not have pushed the button hard enough). ✓ Run the garbage disposal if there is any food in the sink. (Make sure to turn the faucet on before running the disposal and to turn off the disposal first, then the faucet.)

Choose a task and write it on a card (color-coding if you like). Next write in the name of the task, approximate time, the point value, and the age restrictions (if any). Now comes one of the most important and critical parts of the system—instructions. Never assume someone knows how to do a specific task—instead, write clear and concise instructions. The time you put into this will come back to you tenfold. (Likewise, if you skimp on this step, you will greatly regret it later!)

I have found the best way to write instructions is to actually complete the task and stop and write down the process step-by-step. This ensures I do not overlook anything. For example, if one of the tasks was to load the dishwasher, my instructions might look like the example on the previous page.

Make sure to think through any special considerations; for example, if your dishwasher has setting for pots/pans, you may want to create a table for what to pick depending on the dish load. Additionally, if you have anything that does not go in the dishwasher (silver, china, wine glasses) make sure to note these as well.

I cannot stress enough the importance of complete instructions. They allow the "doer" to complete the tasks confidently and competently and will encourage additional teamwork. Take your time in creating these checklists as they will be your "masters." To get a head start on your cards, download my premade templates at www.maketodaymatter.net

On the backside of the card, write the frequency. For example, daily; or Monday, Wednesday, and Friday. There are three columns: date, name, and OK. When someone completes the task they should write the date and their name and then "turn it in" (see system setup in the next section). Once you approve the work and award the points, place a checkmark in the box. The card will last until all of the lines are filled, then you will need to make a new card.

As you finish a card place an X in the "Card Made" column of the Task List Worksheet.

Keeping Track of Points

Use the register provided in this Mini to track points. It works just like a check register; points can be added and subtracted and then the total is carried to the next line. Add points as you approve tasks. Subtract points when they are redeemed by the "doer" or if you are using a repercussion system, subtract points for repercussions.

IMPORTANT: If you choose to use a repercussion system, make sure to spell out how many points will be deducted and for what. Nothing destroys a system that is geared toward positive enforcement faster than a participant not **clearly** understanding why something is taken away. I strongly suggest writing down any repercussions and their points deduction on a page that everyone can consult.

Tip: Keep the register somewhere the participants can easily check their balance.

Setting Up the System

The last step is to set up the system in a visible place. The easiest way is to use catalog envelopes or self-adhesive pockets on a sheet of posterboard, cut to the size of a refrigerator door. Place the cards into pockets based on frequency. If you have separate age groups, place the cards for younger kids closer to the bottom. If you have cards that are not coming up within the next four weeks, keep these stored in a shoe box or in envelopes divided by months.

Have a designated spot for people to turn in cards upon completion. Empty the cards and record the points as needed and then return to the system or the shoebox depending when they are next due. (Consider making this recording process a reward task for kids if you want to delegate it!)

Register

Register
Name:
Points (+ or -)
Date:
Balance
Points (+ or -)
Date:
Balance
Points (+ or -)
Date:
Balance
Points (+ or -)
Date:
Balance
Points (+ or -)
Date:
Balance
Points (+ or -)
Date:
Balance
Points (+ or -)
Date:
Balance
Points (+ or -)
Date:
Balance
Points (+ or -)
Date:
Balance
Points (+ or -)
Date:
Balance

Tip: If you do not want to put this on your refrigerator, consider the back of a main closet door or use a photo album with pockets. You can also use a three-ring binder, with slash pockets and hole-punched envelopes. The binder can stay in a high-traffic area for easy access.

Monthly Refreshing

Once a month check your shoebox or envelopes for any new cards that will be coming due and add them to the system. (You can also assign this Monthly Refreshing as a task!)

Points in Exchange for _____

Before explaining the system to your family, the rewards need to be determined. Here are a few ideas:

- Assign a dollar value to every five points earned. (You can also create incentives for completing more tasks in a week—for example, earn thirty points and receive a bonus of X points.)
- Ask your child what they really want. This can be anything— little or big. Then determine how many points would be needed for the item. This creates a direct correlation for understanding how much work it takes to acquire an item. This method works well for keeping the emphasis on work and reward versus dollars and cents.
- Brainstorm a list of privileges such as choosing the next movie, the restaurant you eat at when dining out, riding in the front seat—whatever it is that your kids often want to have "their way." Assign points based on the privilege.

Explaining the System

Explaining the system is easiest when you have all the components complete. Make sure to have the following determined:

- Tasks to be completed
- How points are earned
- The value chart for points (either use my template or create your own)
- Any quota required (for example, each family member needs to earn five points per week)
- The register to show them
- The system and cards so you can choose where people can pick up cards and where to put them when done
- If using repercussions, have a list of the repercussions and points deducted

---

Tip: *The best results are achieved when everyone works together. Go ahead and put your own routine tasks on cards and keep track of your points! The goal is not to create competition but to foster a spirit of teamwork. Kids are inspired by seeing their parents' involvement. Your consistent achievement will lay a foundation for their own — and besides, I am sure you could think of a few things you might want to redeem points for!*

Monthly Worksheet

Task List Worksheet

Task	Frequency	Time Needed	Difficulty 1 = easy 2 = medium 3 = hard	Age Range	Points Equation	Point Value	Card Made
			1 2 3				
			1 2 3				
			1 2 3				
			1 2 3				
			1 2 3				
			1 2 3				
			1 2 3				
			1 2 3				
			1 2 3				
			1 2 3				
			1 2 3				
			1 2 3				
			1 2 3				
			1 2 3				
			1 2 3				
			1 2 3				
			1 2 3				
			1 2 3				
			1 2 3				
			1 2 3				
			1 2 3				

goals & career

"Shoot for the moon. Even if you miss, you'll land among the stars."
—*Les Brown*

Whether you are in a profession you love, in-between jobs, or pursuing a new passion, you will find Minis in this section to explore your goals and expand your horizons. From mind-mapping to project management to a creative way to pursue goals, you'll learn skills that can help you move past limits and increase productivity.

Mini-Makeovers
- Creating a Goal Grab Bag
- Mind Mapping
- Effective Project Management
- Seven-Day Anti-Stress Regimen

mini-makeover

creating a goal grab bag

"Only those who will risk going too far can possibly find out how far one can go."—*T.S. Eliot*

If you have been discouraged by goals and set them half-heartedly or not at all, then the technique I present in this Mini offers a new approach for creating fun mini goals. You can use this technique to set goals for a week, a month, a quarter, or an entire year. It is a great technique for regaining the focus that flows with life.

Action Step Checklist
- ☐ Complete the Step One reflection question.
- ☐ Brainstorm your action items.
- ☐ Complete the Step Four worksheet.
- ☐ Refresh your Goal Grab Bag as desired.

Statistics reveal New Year resolutions are "out," with less than 50 percent of Americans setting resolutions when the clock strikes midnight. It wasn't long ago that 88 percent of Americans greeted the New Year with resolution, intention, and expectation. What's changed?

Historically, more than 80 percent of resolutions are abandoned by late February, and many women believe they are doomed before they begin. A resolution becomes another pressure in an already pressure-filled life.

As I waited for the clock to strike midnight one year, I was deep in thought about this challenge we face in reaching our goals. With statistics like these, it seemed as though creating a resolution was a way for many people to procrastinate on the very thing they had resolved to do for another year.

In a recent interview, I was asked why people struggle so much with resolutions. While I could give a top-ten list, there is one major obstacle to reaching our goals that I want to help you overcome in this Mini.

Step One: Find Ten Minutes in Your Day

Some of the most common resolutions include exercising daily, going on a new diet, spending more time daily with a loved one, and making X more dollars. While these goals are admirable, they do not always account for the reality of life. Think of the last time you had 365 consecutive days to focus your efforts on the same thing consistently. For me, the answer would be thirty-five years ago, when I was born, and for the first year of my life, my daily focus was likely on getting food and love.

With life being as busy as it is, finding uninterrupted time to focus is a challenge. However, I am confident that all of us can find one thing: ten minutes of focused time per day. Think about it for a minute: where do you have ten minutes that "escape" from you and don't help move you forward? Here are a few places to check:

- Lying in bed versus getting up
- Watching television
- Spending time on the Internet that doesn't move you toward a goal
- Complaining
- Engaging in phone or text-message conversations that aren't refreshing or renewing
- Worrying
- Procrastinating

Think of three to five areas where ten minutes often escape in a way that does not productively move you toward what you want to achieve. Record these in your journal.

Step Two: Replace an Activity

Now that we have found ten minutes, it is time to fill them with an activity that will move us forward in creating the life we want. However, we are not going to choose one activity to do consistently each day. Instead, we are going to create a Goal Grab Bag that is flexible enough to handle our busy lives.

If you are familiar with the monthly Snapshot from the *Change Your Life Challenge* program (CYLC), complete a fresh Snapshot before moving on to the next step. If you are not familiar with this tool, look at the areas that follow, and star the three or four areas you feel most need attention in your life.

Life Areas Needing Attention

Health	Attitude	Self-Time
Energy	Joy	Friendships
Faith	Finances	Time Management
Household	Career	Mealtimes
Relationship w/ children	Relationship w/ significant other	

Please complete this step before continuing.

In your journal, list the Life Areas you starred, leaving about five lines between each entry. Under each heading, list three to five specific ten-minute activities that would move you toward your goals in that Life Area.

Brainstorming Tips
- Feel free to list more than five activities.
- Focus your list on the next sixty to ninety days.
- Make sure your list items are concrete and specific.

Step Three: Create Your Goal Grab Bag
Using the Monthly Goal worksheet on the previous page, go "life-enhancement shopping" by transferring items from your brainstorm list. Move one list item to each row until the sheet is full. If you have extras, save them for the next time you decide to refresh your Goal Grab Bag.

Step Four: Use Your Goal Grab Bag
Each day, choose one item from your Goal Grab Bag list and complete it. Place a check under the applicable column to indicate which item you chose. You are free to do more than one item, <u>but aim to do a minimum of one item at least five to six days per week for maximum impact</u>.

Step Five: Refresh Your Grab Bag
You can make a new Grab Bag each month, each quarter, each year, or each week. Anytime you feel you are losing ground, use this technique to get back to basics and bring focus back into your life.

mini-makeover

mind mapping

"Life is 'trying things to see if they work.'"—*Ray Bradbury*

I have used Mind Maps for the past eighteen years for various purposes. Mind Maps can help us:

- Break through creative blocks
- Discover solutions and new approaches to challenges
- Think "outside the box"
- Brainstorm
- Take notes (great for right-brained learners)
- Break down a project into manageable parts

I'll take you step-by-step through creating a Mind Map and using the technique to accomplish all of the above.

Action Step Checklist

- ☐ Read the six steps to creating a Mind Map.
- ☐ Complete your first Mind Map using one of the provided prompts.
- ☐ Read through the additional Mind Map ideas.
- ☐ Try one of the ideas that appeals to you.
- ☐ Visit the suggested resources for further information.

Mind Maps are most often used to generate, visualize, structure, and classify ideas, and as an aid in study, organization, problem solving, and decision making. Tony Buzan, a pioneer of the Mind Map, claimed that the Mind Map utilizes more of the right and left brain hemispheres. The process of using words and diagrams engages brain attributes that are often not utilized in standard writing. This technique has been successfully applied to note taking for students and brainstorming for companies.

In this Mini we will work through a general Mind Map and then look at ways to apply the technique to other areas.

Tip: Starting a new technique is similar to embarking on a new job or hobby. We go through that unfamiliar period where we don't understand the "lay of the land." As we start with the Mind Map, don't be surprised if you experience the same awkwardness, because this is new and uncharted territory. Expect to work with the technique at least ten times before passing judgment on whether it is beneficial to you.

Six Steps to Creating a Mind Map

I have created a sample Mind Map to walk us through this process. This was recreated on the computer for readability only. I do all my Mind Maps longhand — but you would never be able to read my writing! Refer to this Mind Map as you follow the Mind Mapping instructions.

Step One: Turn Your Paper

Turn your paper to the landscape position. Perhaps because we are not used to writing with our papers in this position, it increases our ability for the free association of ideas.

Tip: For your first map, set a timer for either five or ten minutes after reading through the instructions.

Step Two: Start at the Center
Create a circle in the middle of the page. Write a word or draw an image representing what you want to work with during the exercise (prompts follow). Draw a branch from the center to a main area. Branch out these ideas into more detailed ideas. Try to use a single word for each entry. For example, I used the word "questions" as my prompt and then branched out to "happiness" and "self-discovery."

   Once you have your subject in the middle, draw lines coming from the center relating to that theme. Continue making new branches to follow additional themes. These words and entries don't have to make sense. <u>Just let go and let words tumble out.</u> Don't censor, evaluate, or pass judgment—just let it flow.

Step Three: Keep Going!
As you work, add additional branches. Use these to clarify your thoughts with short phrases or ideas. You can keep expanding from this center for as long as you like. Think of the Mind Map as a "thought explosion" on paper.

Step Four: Circles, Squiggles, Drawings — All Are Welcome!
Do not limit yourself to just circles with connecting lines. If you feel like making a squiggly line, zigzag, double line, or any other shape, go for it! You can also use drawings instead of words. As you continue to use Mind Maps, you may want to explore using different colors, markers, or pencils.

Step Five: Circle Back
Follow a "thought branch" as far as it will take you. As soon as you get stuck, go back to the center word and follow another path. Move to another word whenever you feel like it. While some of the entries may seem irrelevant or senseless, don't worry about that. Over time a series of random entries in Mind Maps can weave together to create an interesting discovery.

Step Six: Connect the Dots

After you create your Mind Map, take a few minutes to review it. Color or highlight any ideas or thoughts that really resonate with you. Look for connections and mark them with arrows. For example, a branch you started on the left may tie into something on the right. Create arrows or highlight a line to connect related ideas. The Mind Map in my example was a starting point for many entries; you can see how each main theme (each shaded area) could be an entry in and of itself. I can also take any of these words and make it the center of a new Mind Map to dig deeper.

Create Your First Mind Map

Turn your paper lengthwise and choose one of these prompts to write in a circle in the middle of the paper:

- The current year (i.e., 2010, 2012)
- Changes
- Questions
- I want to discover…

Now start the process of recording your thoughts and following them where they lead. Continue this exercise for ten minutes. If you find you have run out of room, simply choose any word that captures you from this Mind Map and transfer it to the center of a new page and continue.

More Mapping Techniques

At the start of this Mini, I listed many ways Mind Maps can be used. Now that you have an understanding of the basic process, here are some guidelines and ideas for applying Mind Maps for different purposes.

Double-Time Mind Maps

This method is great for breaking through creative blocks. It can help you discover solutions and new approaches to challenges.

Write the block or challenge in the center circle. Set a timer for two minutes, and generate as many offshoots as you can. When the two minutes have passed, reset the timer for five minutes. Spend this time working from the offshoots created.

Group Maps

Mind Maps can help classify ideas effectively within a group setting.

List the objective in the center. Work around the group, asking each person to offer an idea. List this as the first set of branches. Then continue working around the room to add a second set of branches. Make sure to do this several times so that participants can add to the ideas of others. You can create a Mind Map brainstorm on your own as well. When working on your own, do this as an untimed exercise. Over the period of several days, add new ideas as first branches. Then continue to drill down additional ideas. You could also ask friends or colleagues questions and then add their responses as first branches without ever mentioning you are working on a Mind Map.

Learning and Retention Maps

When in a meeting, class, or other note-taking environment, place the main topic in the center circle (for example, "psychology"). List the main learning points as the first branches. Then continue off these branches with key teaching points. For maximum benefit, after the session, write a brief summary of your Mind Map on the back of your paper to incorporate both right- and left-brain retention ability.

Project Maps

List the project in the center circle. If the project is in development, give each primary objective a branch. Brainstorm second-tier branches to help achieve the objectives. The more complicated the project, the more Mind Maps required. The individual components of primary objectives may require Mind Maps of their own. I have found it helpful to also list resources: Who can assist in this project component? What resources do I need? Give this process as long as you need to cover all your bases. Then transfer the Mind Map into a checklist of action steps.

If the project is already planned and ready to be implemented, then list the project in the center circle. Create first branches containing the central action points—for example, publicity, sales, and presentation. Create additional branches under this first set to capture objectives, and then continue drilling down action steps and resources, adding as many Mind Maps as necessary. When complete, transfer the Mind Map into a checklist of action steps.

Creating a Mind-Map Book

I like to use unlined paper and keep a book of my Mind Maps. Flipping through Mind Maps created over time can really help solve problems, see patterns, and forge new ideas. My Mind-Map Book isn't fancy and is quite simple to put together.

I purchased the following supplies:

- Plain, three-hole-punched paper
- Set of ten thin color markers
- Two-inch binder
- Set of tab dividers
- Zip pocket that fits in the binder

Add a chunk of paper to the binder, and put all the tabs in the back. Place the zip pocket in the front with the markers and a couple of pens so that you don't have to hunt for them each time you want to map.

If you are out and about and choose to Mind Map (which can happen a lot), simply use whatever is handy, and then tape the map on to one of the blank papers in your binder. I have maps on Post-its (not recommended—very hard to read!), napkins, menus, etc.

Use the tab dividers to group like entries together. Let the themes of life determine the divider categories. Once I have a handful of Mind Maps in a given area, I add a tab to keep them grouped together.

Make sure to date all of your entries in the bottom corner and to write a sentence about the topic or question with which you approached that particular Mind Map.

Mind-Mapping Resources

Some people may prefer using a software program or computer to create a map. This is especially beneficial in group environments where a projector is available. The following are some programs to consider.

Online Mind Mapping

Mindomo (www.mindomo.com) offers a free basic account or a paid account with additional features—a good solution for those who want to share Mind Maps remotely. Another option can be found from Mind42 (www.mind42.com).

Free Programs and Shareware

Visit Edraw Soft (www.edrawsoft.com/freemind.php) or FreeMind (freemind.sourceforge.net/wiki/index.php/Main_Page), which offers one of the most comprehensive free programs. At Tucows (www.tucows.com/preview/179836) the download is free, while the shareware cost is ten dollars.

Software with Free Trials

Smart Draw (www.smartdraw.com/specials/mindmapping.asp) is capable of many things; Mind Maps is just one of them.

Additional Links

Wikipedia provides a comprehensive resource of free and professional Mind Mapping programs (en.wikipedia.org/wiki/List_of_mind_mapping_software), as well as details on the history of Mind Mapping and examples and ideas for using Mind Maps in a variety of environments (en.wikipedia.org/wiki/Mind_Map).

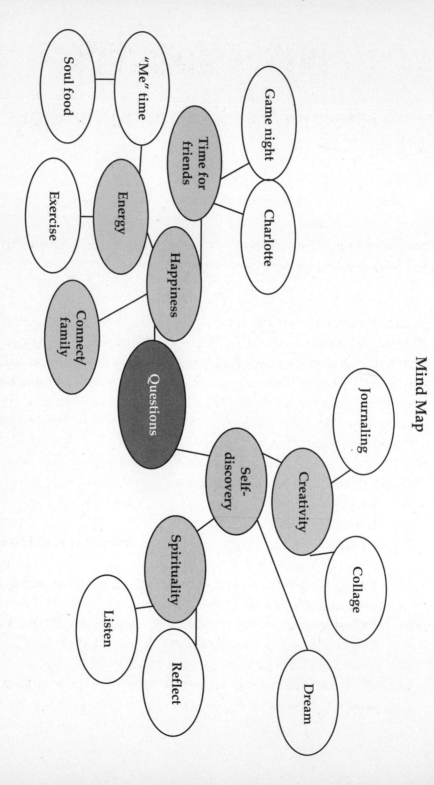

Mind Map

mini-makeover

effective project management

"A plan is a list of actions arranged in whatever sequence is thought likely to achieve an objective."—*John Argenti*

In both careers and goals, most of our to-dos are projects comprised of multiple action steps. Having an efficient system to manage projects helps us stay on course, manage time effectively, and uncover obstacles before we encounter them. Lawrence J. Peter said, "If you don't know where you are going, you will probably end up somewhere else." A solid project plan can take you from where you are to where you want to be.

Action Step Checklist

- ☐ Identify a project.
- ☐ Create a Project Map.
- ☐ Create subproject maps until the project is broken down into actionable steps.
- ☐ Using a calendar to keep other commitments in mind, fill in goal dates for completion.
- ☐ Transfer your main project and subprojects to the Project Overview worksheet at the end of this workbook.
- ☐ Transfer your subproject maps to subproject pages.
- ☐ Add your first action steps to your weekly plan, along with a date to revisit your project to refresh your action list.

Before venturing into project management, it is important to understand the difference between an action step and a project.

A project can be defined as any task requiring more than two steps for completion. For example, doing a load of laundry is a task, or action step, whereas a complete spring cleaning would be a project.

Test Your Project and Task I.Q.

TASK	PROJECT	Running errands
TASK	PROJECT	Sending a birthday card
TASK	PROJECT	Writing a paper
TASK	PROJECT	Cleaning the living room
TASK	PROJECT	Doing taxes
TASK	PROJECT	Picking up a child's toys

Let's test your knowledge on this critical concept before moving forward. Identify each item in the following list by circling either "task" or "project."

Let's see how you did:

- **Running errands** is most often a project because it involves multiple action steps. For example, you might need to gather the dry-cleaning, make a grocery list, call in prescriptions, find photographs to develop, check household inventory, drop off mail, etc.
- **Sending a birthday card** is a task. It involves one or two simple steps: getting the card and mailing it.
- **Writing a paper** is a project, as it is composed of several processes: researching, reading, outlining, writing a rough draft, editing, and finalizing.
- **Cleaning the living room** is a project. It likely involves many tasks like dusting, vacuuming or mopping, picking up odds and ends, cleaning ceiling fixtures, wiping down furniture, etc.
- **Doing taxes** is a project. It likely involves finding the forms

and receipts, calculating totals, filing state, filing federal, seeing a tax professional, etc.

- **Picking up a child's toys** is a task.

Tip: A task can <u>always</u> be completed within a single day.

Types of Projects

Projects can be further broken down by the number of steps they take for completion and the length of time the project spans.

- **Simple:** Any project requiring ten action steps or less can be called a simple project.
- **Complex:** Any project requiring eleven or more action steps is a complex project.
- **Short-Term:** Any project that must be completed within the next sixty days is a short-term project.
- **Long-Term:** Any project with a due date past sixty-one days is a long-term project.

A project then can have one of four different overall types: simple short-term, simple long-term, complex short-term, or complex long-term.

You do not need to memorize this or categorize every project at the get-go; simply be aware that different types of projects require different management and different ground work.

Understanding Due Dates

Every project must have an overall due date, or it risks the chance of not getting done. Some due dates are set externally by others, such as tax deadlines or holiday preparations. If a project does not have an externally set due date, then it is up to you to choose a due date for the project.

A project due date is the date the entire project is to be completed by. The action steps within the project will have different due dates, but the project due date represents the date <u>all action steps</u> will be completed. If you are completely unsure of what to pick for a due date or find that you tend to overestimate when you can complete a project, work backward. Use the planning tools in this Mini to lead you to a projected completion date.

Choosing a Project

The project management routines and techniques you will learn in this Mini require strategic thinking and planning; therefore you may not want to do every step for every project. After learning the process, we will discuss how to handle less complex projects using some of the steps.

To maximize this Mini, I recommend choosing a complex short-term project and then applying each step in-depth to build a solid understanding of project management. Once you have mastered the techniques with one project, you can double back and expand on other projects.

> *A complex short-term project is a project that has a due date within the next sixty days and requires eleven or more individual action steps to complete.*

Project Mapping: Part One

Since we are working with a complex project, the first step in management is to break the project down into manageable components. I have found that Mind Mapping can easily be used effectively for Project Mapping.

Popularized by Tony Buzan, Mind Maps abandon the list format of conventional planning and note taking in favor of a two-dimensional structure. This practice offers a more thorough and well-rounded way of thinking through a project to reveal the overall shape of a project as well as the importance of individual components and their relation to one another. (For more information on how to use Mind Maps, refer to the Mind-Mapping Mini in this book.)

How to Create Your First Project Map
At the top of a blank sheet of paper, make a circle or square and write the project you have chosen in the shape. Leave enough space

to write a sentence or two describing what this project looks like when it is complete—and be specific. Here are a few examples.

- **Project: Create a marketing plan for my home-based business.** This plan will include a detailed outline and implementation schedule for creating marketing collateral, setting up a website, building an online newsletter, creating a press release, and analyzing, choosing, and implementing the best outreach possibilities.
- **Project: Create a household management system.** This plan will include a detailed breakdown of all the home maintenance tasks to be completed on a weekly, monthly, quarterly, and annual basis, as well as a list of who is responsible and a realistic plan for completing these tasks.
- **Project: Redo the basement.** This project encompasses a complete overhaul of the basement to purge the old, maximize space through better organization, and clean thoroughly.
- **Project: Move photographs to scrapbooks.** This plan will take me step by step through organizing photos, deciding on my scrapbook subjects, utilizing on-hand materials, creating a shopping plan for what I need, and developing a timeline for working on the scrapbooks.

Project Mapping: Part Two

We now have the top level of our Project Map. The next step is to take our "project purpose" and break it into key components. Each component should receive its own branch off of the initial shape.

For this example I will use the "create a marketing plan for my home-based business" project, as it is one of the more complex projects on this list. Using this project, my Project Map might look like the example on the next page.

As I begin to lay the project out in this way, I can more clearly see the relationship between the individual components of the project. For example, creating an online newsletter would not be a logical first step because I would need a website first.

> **Tip:** *If you find that you are doing a lot of erasing or changing of "what goes where," use adhesive notes or index cards instead. You can move these around quickly and easily to create your structure and then put it into chart form.*

Project Map

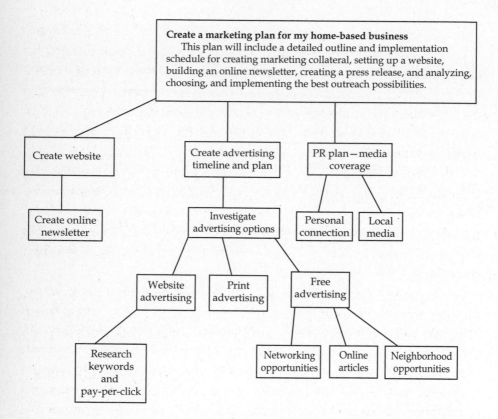

Think of Project Mapping as a two-stage process: The first pass involves creating an "overall map." The second involves delving into further detail. For example, at this point I have created three primary subprojects:

- Create website
- Create advertising timeline and plan
- Strategize public relations (PR) coverage

Because this is a complex project, I will need to dig deeper; if it were a simple project, this one pass might be enough.

Each of these three primary subcategories will likely need its own map if I truly want to understand all the components. Let's look at how this might work with the "create website" subproject. Page 160 offers an example.

Take a look at the chart. Do you see any problems? One of the boxes specifically stands out to me as not an action item. Can you find it?

It's "create hard-copy pages," which would involve basically typing my website up first. I need to understand my navigation and then also create each page before I can make hard copies. If I have a small website or have all the information I need in other files already, perhaps this could remain an action step. However, without that information, this would be better treated as another subproject. In that diagram, I would identify the pages I need to create and the navigation structure.

This level of detail is vital because it helps us prioritize and bring logical order to a project. By creating these maps, I can begin to see relationships between the components. For example, in the advertising and PR subprojects I need to have (1) a place to send potential customers (a website), and (2) something to offer (specific product or content on the website).

I can quickly deduce that the website branch is the first priority, because the other subcategories are dependent on it. If I were to begin with any other category, I would likely have to rework my plan.

> **Remember:** *You need to get down to the individual <u>actionable steps</u> in order to take effective, decisive, and focused action. Create as many subproject levels as necessary to get to the actionable steps. The reason most projects fail or stall is that we don't dig down to the actionable items.*

It's About Time

This exercise has provided me with a logical entrance point into my project: the website branch. With my project beginning to take shape, I will need to add some goal dates for completing the individual project components.

Create Website

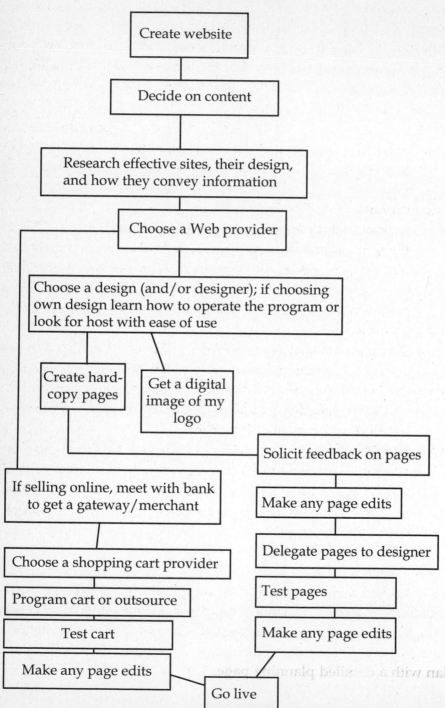

Before I can do that, I need to approximate how long the steps will take so I can realistically fit them into my schedule. First I will write in the time I think I need <u>plus</u> a 30 percent cushion, since studies show that we tend to underestimate how long a specific task will take. For example, if I believe I can complete a task in an hour, I will allot one hour and twenty minutes. To start, I will add these estimates to my maps in pencil.

With my time approximations set, I can now add goal dates. Again I will do this in pencil, as things often change while completing the planning process.

Three Important Time Tips

- **Action Check:** Before adding dates and time approximations, make sure your map has been broken down into actual action steps. It is much easier to create an accurate goal date for a specific task than for a group of tasks. By choosing a goal date for individual tasks and working up the branch, we create a more realistic overall time plan.
- **Overage Check:** Remember to calculate a 30 percent overage—minimum. Even if you don't think you need it, amuse me. The project-planning worksheets you complete will help you discover your personal overage percentage, but in the interim use 30 percent.
- **Life Check:** It is handy to have your task lists and calendar nearby when planning a project, because you need time to take action. Consider the time of year, holidays, outside commitments, and all the irons in the fire to ensure as realistic a plan as possible.

From Map to Plan

This map has now created a solid template for a plan—only one problem: it would be difficult to use these maps to effectively track, manage, and implement the project. The maps are a tool to help us see the whole picture of a project, but now we need to firm up the plan with a detailed planning page.

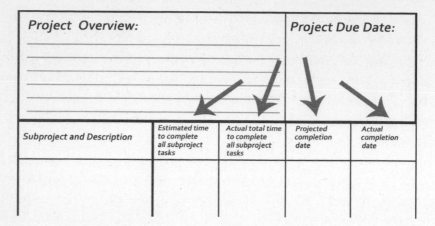

Project Overview:			Project Due Date:	
Subproject and Description	Estimated time to complete all subproject tasks	Actual total time to complete all subproject tasks	Projected completion date	Actual completion date

Creating the Project Overview

At the top of the project overview page, rewrite your project description. Following this space you will see a subproject planning grid. Transfer your Project Map categories to this chart along with your estimated schedule.

Note the columns to estimate the time needed for your subproject and the action time taken. If your plan veers off course, these numbers often reveal the source. They also allow a quick view of how accurate your ability is to estimate time, a skill that is invaluable for planning future projects and delivering on your target date.

Project-Support Pages

Each subproject will likely require a page of its own. The project-support pages offer a grid to transfer all of your Project Map findings. When you transfer your subprojects to these pages, place one subproject on each page with the action steps that follow. It is very important that these be individual <u>action steps</u>.

FAQ: What if what I have written down on my Project Map isn't an action step?

You aren't done yet! Keep breaking it down. You know you have an action step when it meets all three of these criteria:

1. *The task can be completed in one primary location.*
2. *The task can be completed in a single day.*
3. *The task itself is not overwhelming.*

The subproject planning pages are very similar to the overall project page, except that they also include a "priority" column in the top corner. It is important to prioritize a project, and the mapping technique helps us do that by viewing project dependencies. I like to number my subprojects in order—i.e., one, two, three, four—with "one" indicating the subproject to begin with.

The other difference is that the subproject pages have a "delegation" area. Often projects require the help of another person. Perhaps we have dropped something off and will need to pick it up or have outsourced a piece of our project and are awaiting a response. Use this space to record and track those steps.

Delegation Chart

Delegated To: (include contact info)	Description:	Follow up on:	Due Date:
Key Information (contacts, emails, account numbers, etc.)			

Working the Plan

Imagine an architect creating a blueprint for a home she has planned to build. She arrives at the construction site and meets the builders; however, she has forgotten her blueprint. Pressed for time as she is, which of the following do you think she would say, "Don't worry, guys. I have it mapped out and remember a lot of it, so let's just wing it," or "I'll go back and get my blueprint"?

If she plans to remain in the architecture field, I would imagine she would pick the second option. This brings us to the key to success: a plan will be effective only if it is <u>used</u>.

How often you consult your plan will depend on the plan itself. Some plans require daily consult, others weekly, and others somewhere in between. After completing your plan, schedule your first action steps into your week and also schedule the best time to revisit your plan for your next steps.

Revise, Don't Abandon

One important thing to understand about project planning is how rarely things go according to plan. Building in the 30 percent time allowance is a great step in combating plan derailment. While I recommend writing in pen on your actual project-planning worksheets (this increases commitment), you may want to use pencil the first few go-rounds for easy adjustments. By recording your time estimates and how long your action steps and projects actually take to complete, you will reveal your personal overage percentage. Use this number when creating plans in the future instead of the baseline of 30 percent.

You may discover, as I have, that my overage is different for different types of projects. For example, with writing projects I can usually work with a 10 percent overage. When it comes to web projects, I often have to allot 50 percent. Watch for trends in time estimation by type of project.

How to Regroup

Schedule some quiet time to look at your map and planning worksheets. Identify specifically where you veered off course. Then consider the following questions:

- Was this course change necessary because I learned something new, causing my path to change, or was this course change due to something project-related I did not foresee?

- Does this change bring to mind any other possible items to consider as I revamp my plan?
- Do I need to build in additional overage time to my overall plan?

Keep all of your observations with your other project papers. These observations offer valuable clues to improving your project management skills. After answering these questions, revamp your plan based on your findings.

> *Tip:* I like to use a three-ring binder to manage projects. I keep the overview page in a sheet protector and then place the supporting subproject pages behind it. I usually add a paper slash pocket folder to hold any miscellaneous paper along with a color-coded multi-capacity sheet protector. I store smaller projects in one binder, divided by tabs, and larger projects in a binder of their own.

Project Worksheet

Project Overview:	Project Due Date

Subproject and Description	Est. Total Time to Complete All Sub-project Tasks	Actual Total Time to Complete All Sub-project Tasks	Projected Completion Date	Actual Completion Date

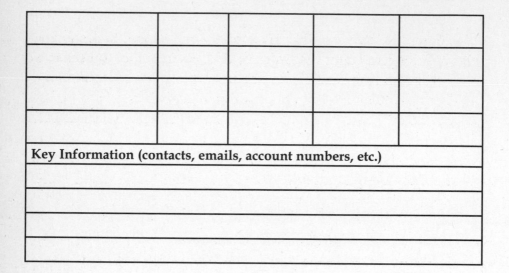

Key Information (contacts, emails, account numbers, etc.)

Regroup Analysis

Project: _____

Date: _____

Was this course change necessary because I learned something new, causing my path to change, or was this course change due to something project-related I did not foresee?

_____

_____

_____

_____

Does this change bring to mind any other possible items to consider as I revamp my plan?

_____

_____

_____

_____

Do I need to build in additional overage time to my overall plan?

_____

_____

What other resources could I utilize to help me? (Could I ask someone who has done something similar for tips? Read a book on the topic at hand? Team up with a family member or friend? Delegate more? Let go of perfection?) Try to brainstorm at least five.

_____

_____

_____

_____

Subproject Worksheet

Subproject Description			Due Date	Priority
Action Step	Est. Time to Complete (Hours/ Minutes)	Actual Time to Complete (Hours/ Minutes)	Projected Completion Date	Actual Completion Date

mini-makeover

seven-day anti-stress regimen

"The kindest thing you can do for the people you care about is to become a happy, joyous person."—*Brian Tracy*

The American Psychological Association recently reported that 79 percent of people believe "stress is a way of life." And nearly half of Americans believe their stress has increased in the last five years, negatively impacting their personal and professional lives. Stress takes a physical and emotional toll if we do not proactively manage it. In this Mini we will work through a Seven-Day Anti-Stress Regimen.

Action Step Checklist
- ☐ Complete Day One of the Anti-Stress Regimen.
- ☐ Complete Day Two of the Anti-Stress Regimen.
- ☐ Complete Day Three of the Anti-Stress Regimen.
- ☐ Complete Day Four of the Anti-Stress Regimen.
- ☐ Complete Day Five of the Anti-Stress Regimen.
- ☐ Complete Day Six of the Anti-Stress Regimen.
- ☐ Complete Day Seven of the Anti-Stress Regimen.

When we experience stress, it is often because something is pressing or because we are overwhelmed with to-dos and projects or because a relationship needs time that we can't find. When pressure reaches its peak, we carve out time to handle a particular stressor. Any guesses on where we most often carve that time from?

We tend to pick up the necessary time by neglecting healthy habits such as relaxation, healthy meals, and exercise. While this might seem a solution in the short term, it is actually a catch-22: By skipping healthy habits, we reduce our physical and emotional energy, making it harder to cope with the stressful situation. So what's a gal to do? While eliminating all stress would be ideal, it isn't a realistic solution. Since we can't eliminate it, we need to learn to manage it. Proactively minimizing stress and increasing our coping abilities can drastically reduce the impact of stress on our lives.

Studies have linked stress to headaches, heart disease, intensifying existing asthma, gastrointestinal problems, fatigue, and chronic pain.

While you might feel your number-one commitment is to your family, a passion, a vision, or another factor, we all share the same number-one commitment, and that is a commitment to self-care and self-nurturing.

Do not begin reading more quickly or skipping this section altogether while thinking, "Yeah, right. Where would I find time for that?" I used to think that way, and my inefficiency showed it. The more I fought this universal truth, the more difficult my life was to manage.

Finding time for self isn't an option; it's a necessity.

Women are nurturers by nature. This is a wonderful and necessary quality, but it has a dangerous downside. When we are too busy caring for others, we put self-care at the bottom of the list. While this may seem "admirable" or "noble," we aren't doing anyone any favors, especially those we are trying to care for. No matter how "strong" you believe yourself to be, or how independent, or how "different" than other women, you need to rejuvenate. Some women only take time to rejuvenate when they find themselves down, in a funk, or worn out. By practicing self-care regularly, we can avoid many funks.

Think of your life as a pitcher of caring. Each time you care and nurture, you pour some of this kindness on to others. If you refill it once a month, you will have to ration small portions to cover everyone, or you will run out early in the month. If you refill it once a week, you can nurture a bit more, but you will still have to use caution to make sure you have enough to go around. The only way to fill this pitcher is by recharging. When recharging is done daily, we feed our own souls and fill the pitcher to care for others in the process. In addition to affecting those we care for, the fullness of this pitcher affects everything in our life, from hobbies to work to home.

You are not a bottomless supply house of caring and energy: you can only give what you have. Would you expect your car to drive nonstop without refueling and maintenance? Of course not. Are you expecting yourself to run nonstop without refueling and maintenance? If you were a car, when was the last time you stopped for gas, had your oil changed, had your windows wiped clean? If you were a car, would you be worn out or rusted due to poor maintenance?

Very few people I know would buy a new car and run it into the ground without maintenance. Very few people could afford to do that. What is more valuable: your life or a new car? What gets better care: your life or your car?

At least five days each week, schedule a minimum of ten minutes, preferably twenty, to focus on *you*. Many people wonder, what should I do during this time? The answer: whatever you want. You do not need to decide today. When the scheduled time arrives, ask yourself, *what would refuel me today?* Some days it might be a walk. Other days it might be a coffee or a trip to a card shop. Some days you may want to nap or just read a book. There isn't a "proper" activity. The only guideline is to reserve this time for you and you alone. All your energy and attention is undivided and aimed at yourself versus others.

These rejuvenation periods need to be a routine commitment. Each week, mark this time off in your calendar before adding other items. I cannot emphasize this enough, so let me say it one more time: If you choose not to do this, please do not expect any major changes in your life to last. While you may experience a flash of energy, ultimately you will be the car sitting on the side of the road, waiting for a tow.

Seven-Day Anti-Stress Regimen

As you work to implement your Action Plan, remember that stress does not evaporate overnight. However, in each moment we can take proactive action to change our focus and look at what we <u>can</u> do instead of what we <u>can't</u> do.

Each day follow the instructions for reducing your stressors. The techniques focus on behaviors to minimize future stressors as well as on reframing perspective and handling current stressors.

Day One: Find Fifteen Unstressful Minutes
Think of this as an order from your doctor—no excuses. It doesn't matter what you do as long as you are not stressed while doing it. Write down what activity you did for your stress-free fifteen minutes here:

_____

Day Two: Ask Questions
Each time you feel stress today, ask yourself, What really needs to be done? Can I make any adjustments to make this less stressful? Is there anything I can do right now to make a dent in this? Articulate your answer in a single sentence, then act. Don't hesitate—doing so will stress you out.

My results:

_____
_____
_____
_____
_____

Day Three: Compromise

Today when you are feeling stressed, compromise instead of confronting, if appropriate. Sometimes being right only leads to more stress. (This is true whether you're dealing with another person or just with yourself!) Choose to affirm instead of argue (either with yourself or someone else). The Mental Health Association offers this wisdom: "If you find you're meeting constant opposition in either your personal or professional life, rethink your position or strategy. Arguing only intensifies stressful feelings. If you know you are right, stand your ground, but do so calmly and rationally. Make allowances for others' opinions and be prepared to compromise. If you are willing to give in, others may meet you halfway. Not only will you reduce your stress, you may find better solutions to your problems."

My results:

_____

_____

_____

_____

_____

Day Four: Practice Relaxing

Whether you have a lot of stress in your life or you've got it under control, you can benefit from learning relaxation techniques. Science shows relaxation increases blood flow to major muscles, lowers blood pressure, slows heart rate, and reduces muscle tension. All of these benefits will equip you to better handle daily stressors. Learning basic relaxation techniques isn't hard. Complete one of the relaxing exercises detailed here today. Then continue this relaxation exercise over the course of your Anti-Stress Regimen.

Deep breathing is a good way to relax. Here's how to do it:

- Lie down or sit in a chair.
- Rest your hands on your stomach.
- Slowly count to five as you inhale through your nose. Feel your stomach rise.

- Slowly count to five while exhaling through your mouth. (Try to count at the same pace on both the inhale and exhale. If five is difficult, use three.)
- Repeat five times.

The Mayo Clinic offers a nice overview of techniques to help reduce stress (www.mayoclinic.com/print/relaxation-technique/ SR00007/METHOD=print). Among the techniques is the **progressive muscle relaxation technique**, which is what I use at the end of each day. Mayo experts explain it this way: "In this technique, you focus on slowly tensing and then relaxing each muscle group. This helps you focus on the difference between muscle tension and relaxation, and you become more aware of physical sensations. You may choose to start by tensing and relaxing the muscles in your toes and progressively working your way up to your neck and head. Tense your muscles for at least five seconds and then relax for thirty seconds, and repeat."

I do each muscle group three times, beginning with toes, then progressing through feet, calves, thighs, buttocks, torso/stomach, chest, hands, arms, shoulders, neck, and then head. I hold clenched for five to ten seconds on the inhale (while slowly counting to five or ten) and then exhale and relax for equal seconds, repeating each muscle group three times before moving upward in my body. Counting slowly helps to keep the mind "less busy." I learned this technique as a young child when I was having problems falling asleep due to nightmare anxiety.

The first time I did this, someone walked me through the exercise. (You can create a similar effect by reciting this exercise into a tape player while also playing soothing music in the background. Then listen to the "walk-through" on a headset while lying in bed. This helps to free up the mind as well.) The first time I did it, I think I made it to my stomach before falling asleep. Even to this day, I rarely make it past shoulders—which is the whole point! It is so relaxing it helps prepare the body for sleep and/or deep relaxation. The key is to hold each muscle group as tightly as possible for the full count and then exhale—and to do so slowly. Also, place one hand over your abdomen to make sure you are breathing deeply from your stomach versus breathing from your chest. You will know if this is occurring because your abdomen will be moving instead of your chest.

> **Tip:** *You can also use this exercise while sitting in a chair as a way to induce rest for a refreshing power nap.*

My results:

_____

_____

_____

_____

_____

Day Five: Talk to Someone

Talk to your friends to help you work through your stress, or just talk to your friends to do something other than sit in your stress. Instead of thinking about your challenges, talk about them. This can really help put them in perspective. Find someone who is positive-natured and nonjudgmental. There is great value in hearing other perspectives. Today take at least ten minutes to talk versus think.

My results:

_____

_____

_____

_____

_____

Day Six: Cut the Criticism

The Mental Health Association shares this common stress producer: "You may expect too much of yourself and others. Try not to feel frustrated, let down, disappointed, or even 'trapped' when another person does not measure up. The 'other person' may be a wife, a husband, or a child whom you are trying to change to suit yourself. Remember, everyone is unique and has his or her own virtues, shortcomings, and right to develop as an individual." Today your stress challenge is to not criticize, judge, or measure anyone—including yourself!

My results:

_____

_____

_____

_____

_____

_____

Day Seven: Dream, Don't Dwell

Each time you find yourself thinking about a stressful event, redirect your mind to a daydream. Visualize the result you would like. Think about the solution—not the problem. Visualize yourself handling a stressful situation with poise, control, confidence, and grace.

My results:

_____

_____

_____

_____

_____

_____

If you have worked through these exercises, you are well on your way to proactively reducing stress. Continue to work with these activities to keep stress at bay. Whenever you find stress resurfacing, remember to stop and audit the stress, then take action and reframe your thinking.

Is Stress Giving You a Headache? *Research has found that it is actually the day-to-day stress or chronic "hassles" that are important in triggering headache. Compared to men, women often experience more of the types of stress that provoke headache. You can learn more about stress and headaches at the American Council for Headache Education website (www.achenet.org/women/stress).*

Additional Resources

Help may be as close as a friend or spouse. But if you think that you or someone you know may be under more stress than just dealing with a passing difficulty, it may be helpful to talk with your doctor, pastor, or employee-assistance professional. They may suggest you visit with a psychiatrist, psychologist, social worker, or other qualified counselor. Please remember that seeking additional help is not a sign of weakness; it's a sign of strength! It takes courage to deal with a challenge proactively instead of "sweeping it under the rug." Whenever I face an upheaval in life that I am not sure how to deal with, my first stop is a psychotherapist. These are professionals trained to help. I consider it much more efficient to meet the challenge head-on with experts to help generate ideas. I also believe strongly that I owe it to myself, my family, and my readers and community to proactively take care of myself. Please remember that all psychotherapists are not created equal; it may take a few visits to find one that is a match for you. Don't be shy in saying, "This isn't what I am looking for. Might you suggest someone that is _____" — and list the qualities you are looking for. A good psychotherapist will not be offended, as the goal is to help you in the most efficient manner.

The National Institutes of Health suggests the following points to consider when talking with a professional:

- List the things that cause stress and tension in your life.
- How does this stress and tension affect you, your family, and your job?
- Can you identify the stress and tensions in your life as short or long term?
- Do you have a support system of friends or family that will help you make positive changes?
- What are your biggest obstacles to reducing stress?
- What are you willing to change or give up for a less stressful and tension-filled life?
- What have you tried already that didn't work for you?
- If you do not have control of a situation, can you accept it and get on with your life?

The National Institute of Mental Health and National Institutes of Health have put together a simple online PowerPoint presentation to help explain stress more effectively. You can view this PowerPoint at www.nlm.nih.gov/medlineplus/tutorials/managingstress/htm/index.htm.

time & information management

"Don't say you don't have enough time. You have exactly the same number of hours per day that were given to Helen Keller, Pasteur, Michelangelo, Mother Teresa, Leonardo da Vinci, Thomas Jefferson, and Albert Einstein."—*H. Jackson Brown, Jr.*

Like it or not, we all have the same twenty-four hours in a day. While people often exclaim they do not have enough time, often what is meant is that they do not have enough direction or focus. In this section we explore techniques to help us direct our focus to make the most of our days.

Mini-Makeovers
- The Ten Faces of Procrastination
- Overcoming Magazine Madness: Creating a Personal Reference Library
- Little Time Blocks
- Reality Routines

mini-makeover

the ten faces of procrastination

"Only put off until tomorrow what you are willing to die having left undone."—*Pablo Picasso*

The number of tasks that pile up on our "someday list" is often a prime stressor and joy drainer. Understanding how and why we put off specific tasks can unlock action and focus.

Action Step Checklist

- ☐ Answer Reflection Questions #1 and #2.
- ☐ Complete the Procrastination Quiz.
- ☐ Complete column A of the Top Five worksheet.
- ☐ Complete column B of the Top Five worksheet.
- ☐ Write your Prescription for Procrastination.

Many people believe that procrastination is a result of poor planning or poor time management. Others believe it is a lack of organizational skills. Some believe it is a lack of focus, ability, or willpower. All of these beliefs are **false.**

Each of these beliefs deals with the external—how procrastination appears on the surface—but none of these beliefs deal with the source or root cause of procrastination. Let's take a detailed look at what happens in the mind of the procrastinator through this eight-phase cycle I have designed.

The Eight-Phase Cycle

This is what procrastination looks like:

1. You want to achieve an outcome. Often this is something that either you personally place a high value on or the people you admire or respect place a high value on. Regardless, you feel an internal need to start.
2. Prior to starting, you weigh the pros and cons. (The result of this evaluation varies greatly depending on your personal experiences.)
3. One of the cons sets off an emotional response (whether you are aware of it or not). You put off taking action today for tomorrow (or another day) when things will be "better."
4. During this delay, you become more self-critical, and the negative emotional response gains strength.
5. You begin criticizing yourself, saying, "I should have started already," "Anybody could do this," "What is wrong with me?" Or you create another distraction or obligation (real or imagined) as an excuse for not taking action.
6. The task hits crisis level, where you either (a) do it hastily, (b) throw your hands up in frustration, or (c) procrastinate on yet another item so you can get this crisis-level task completed.
7. You beat yourself up for not taking action sooner, feeling you didn't do well enough to prepare. You vow to change your ways.
8. You repeat this eight–step cycle, almost immediately, on another task until it becomes a "way of living."

When we complete this cycle many times and it becomes a "way of living," we begin experiencing procrastination in many areas of our lives. It isn't just cleaning or organization, but cards are sent late, presents are purchased late, many tasks and activities are slated for "someday." You've likely heard the quote, "Someday isn't a day of the week."

Reflection Question #1: Where in Your Life Have You Seen This Eight-Phase Cycle?

Procrastinators
- *believe there is time to do something tomorrow, even though there is time today;*
- *convince themselves they "work best under pressure" or "circumstances will be better for this tomorrow";*
- *tend to overestimate their ability to complete things and thus quickly take on an overwhelming to-do list;*
- *convince themselves that something is unimportant to avoid the guilt that procrastination brings;*
- *often look for distractions (such as perpetually checking email).*

Reflection Question #2: Which of These Beliefs Do You Relate To?

The good news is that we are not born procrastinators—we become them. And anything we learn, we can unlearn. Uncovering your procrastination personality is the first step in that process.

Your Procrastination Quiz

- **Instructions:** Answer honestly—even if you don't like your answers! And whatever you do, please don't procrastinate taking the quiz!
- **Key:** 5 Strongly Agree; 4 Agree; 3 Kinda/Sorta Agree; 2 Disagree; 1 Strongly Disagree

Procrastination Quiz

Section One					
I often feel a rush when completing things at the last minute.	5	4	3	2	1
I tend to have more energy when working under tight deadlines.	5	4	3	2	1
For me, deadlines produce positive stress instead of negative stress.	5	4	3	2	1
I am much more likely to complete a task with a definitive deadline.	5	4	3	2	1
I regularly work (either in the workforce or at home) more than sixty hours per week.	5	4	3	2	1
Section Two					
I am concerned with how others perceive me.	5	4	3	2	1
If I had to choose "not trying" over "trying and failing," I would choose "not trying."	5	4	3	2	1
I often wonder if I have the ability to complete a task on my list.	5	4	3	2	1
When tackling a task, I often wonder if I am doing it "right."	5	4	3	2	1
I find I spend more time thinking about a task than I spend doing it.	5	4	3	2	1
Section Three					
When I am procrastinating, I often spend that time with family and friends.	5	4	3	2	1
Many times when I have procrastinated, it was because I thought something else would make me happier in the moment.	5	4	3	2	1
I place a high value on what others think of me.	5	4	3	2	1
I have wondered if I have a low self-esteem.	5	4	3	2	1
My life is not very balanced, and I get sidetracked easily.	5	4	3	2	1
Section Four					
I have a difficult time making decisions.	5	4	3	2	1
I have a difficult time breaking a large task into smaller actionable steps.	5	4	3	2	1

After making a decision, I worry about whether or not I made the right choice.	5	4	3	2	1
I like to gather a lot of information and do research before making a decision or taking action.	5	4	3	2	1
People have told me that I overanalyze situations (or I feel I overanalyze by thinking too much instead of acting).	5	4	3	2	1

Section Five

I often need instructions or ideas to get started on a task.	5	4	3	2	1
I work better in a group versus independently.	5	4	3	2	1
Often I get upset by the lack of help from _____ (spouse, family, colleagues—fill in the blank).	5	4	3	2	1
I feel I would be able to overcome procrastination if _____ (fill in the blank with anything *external*).	5	4	3	2	1
I often use the excuse, "I will do this after _____." (Fill in the blank with any reason of your choosing.)	5	4	3	2	1

Section Six

I am used to making my own schedule.	5	4	3	2	1
I often do things "my way," and people might describe me as unique, driven, or rebellious.	5	4	3	2	1
I trust that I will know when the best time to complete a task is.	5	4	3	2	1
I like to spend time alone.	5	4	3	2	1
I often experience "high times" when I can get a lot done with very little help.	5	4	3	2	1

Section Seven

I have a fear of rejection or abandonment.	5	4	3	2	1
I do not like to spend time alone.	5	4	3	2	1
I feel better when I work on a task or activity with someone I like versus working independently.	5	4	3	2	1
People have told me I am overly sensitive.	5	4	3	2	1
Sometimes I feel my friends and family have become the focus of my life—to the point where I have very little identity otherwise.	5	4	3	2	1

Section Eight					
I would label myself a perfectionist.	5	4	3	2	1
I take on more commitments than is humanly possible to complete.	5	4	3	2	1
I have a difficult time saying no.	5	4	3	2	1
I often feel overwhelmed and don't know where to begin.	5	4	3	2	1
I like to have structure to my days and become restless with too much unstructured time.	5	4	3	2	1
Section Nine					
I often start projects but don't finish them.	5	4	3	2	1
I often have bursts of energy and set goals during those bursts—only to fizzle out later.	5	4	3	2	1
I am disorganized.	5	4	3	2	1
People tell me I am extremely creative.	5	4	3	2	1
I am easily distracted.	5	4	3	2	1
Section Ten					
I feel exhausted when I look at my to-do list.	5	4	3	2	1
When I look at my current and historic inventory, I begin to feel bad about myself.	5	4	3	2	1
I think this program might work for others, but as for me—I need a miracle.	5	4	3	2	1
I have a very low energy level and require more than eight hours of sleep to feel rested—and even then, I'm often not rested.	5	4	3	2	1
I have purchased—and abandoned—many self-improvement programs, courses, or audio tapes.	5	4	3	2	1

Please total your scores for each section:			
Section One:	**Section Two:**	**Section Three:**	**Section Four:**
Section Five:	**Section Six:**	**Section Seven:**	**Section Eight:**
Section Nine:	**Section Ten:**		

The Top Five

Before we analyze your quiz findings, we have one important inventory to complete. Note the projects, tasks, or to-dos on which you are currently procrastinating. Make sure to list five. List these out in column A. We will return to column B after interpreting the quiz results.

Column A	Column B

Interpreting Your Quiz Results: The Ten Procrastination Personality Types

Each of the ten areas in the quiz details a specific type of procrastination personality. The higher your score in an area, the more likely you are to experience the roadblocks and emotional reactions of that personality.

Most people will fall into multiple categories. However, we need to look at each category independently in order to discover the source and reprogram for success. Sometimes we may find that specific personality types apply to specific types of tasks. We may commonly exhibit two of the personality types in work affairs and two different types in home affairs.

Section One Score: The Adrenaline Junkie

This person experiences a euphoric rush when doing things at the last minute—and getting them done! However, the adrenaline that accompanies tight deadlines isn't consistent. When the energy doesn't emerge, deadlines pass. This person commonly enjoys being the center of attention and performing "heroically" at the last minute. You might hear this person say, "I stayed up two nights in a row to finish this project!"

The Adrenaline Junkie finds excitement and motivation in "pulling off the impossible." An Adrenaline Junkie is often better at managing big projects than day-to-day affairs. She appreciates challenge and finds day-to-day to-dos monotonous or boring. Often she will transform simple to-dos into more impressive feats. For example, she may wait until the last minute to complete a registration to add "excitement" to the process.

While a sense of great accomplishment follows a completed task, an equal amount of self-directed negativity occurs when a task is not completed—and more often than not, at least half of them aren't. After all, if all the tasks could be completed easily, there wouldn't be an adrenaline rush.

- **Reduce commitments.** The Adrenaline Junkie needs to clearly prioritize and be cautious in time delegation. She will often fill her schedule to the brim to create the adrenaline and pressure she seeks.
- **Disconnect commitments and confidence.** There are other ways to create excitement without the risk of self-directed negativity. In addition, the Adrenaline Junkie needs to seek out other confidence builders, rather than deriving the majority of her confidence from superhuman last-minute feats.

Section Two Score: The Avoidant Procrastinator

This person might fear success, failure, or both. Whatever the motivator, she is concerned by how others perceive her and would rather be seen as lacking effort than ability.

- **Remember actions do not equal self-worth.** Often an Avoidant Procrastinator believes she has failed in the past or let someone down. This person needs to learn that actions alone do not create self-worth.

- **Focus on passion- and purpose-driven tasks.** At least one goal or project on the Avoidant Procrastinator's list should inspire energy and passion. This helps move past the "immobile" phase that commonly accompanies this type.
- **Face the fears.** Whether the motivator is fear of success or fear of failure, it needs to be confronted. If we hold onto our fears, they hold onto us — creating a barrier between us and life.
- **Start with little, little steps.** When we fail to deliver on a task or goal, we need to evaluate our planning ability. An Avoidant Procrastinator needs to break projects down into microscopic, attainable steps. Through this level of detail, she can enjoy daily successes, gain momentum, and see that the past need not control the present.

Section Three Score: The Pleasure Seeker

The Pleasure Seeker doesn't want to get her hands dirty. She perpetually lives "in the moment," doing what makes her happy at the time and avoiding unpleasant tasks. Often this type of procrastinator lacks self-esteem and ties much of her self-esteem to interactions with others and approval of peers.

A Pleasure Seeker has often been reprimanded or criticized throughout her life. A natural tendency to avoid pain and seek pleasure is apparent.

- **Build self-worth.** Learning to derive pleasure through successful completion of tasks rather than avoiding tasks is important to balance this type.
- **Cultivate discipline.** The Pleasure Seeker is often diverted from a task and takes off in another direction. Developing discipline to stick to a project is necessary to avoid the impulsiveness that accompanies this personality type.

Section Four Score: The Indecisive Procrastinator

The Indecisive Procrastinator struggles and ultimately doesn't make a decision. Avoiding decisions relinquishes her from responsibility, blame, and accountability. This person often dislikes confrontation of any kind and is very sensitive to the words and actions of others.

- **Evaluate pros and cons.** The Indecisive Procrastinator has to build confidence in her decision-making skills. Learning to carefully weigh pros and cons and having someone to "bounce things off of" can help this person make decisions.
- **Experience the rewards of responsibility.** While not having responsibility reduces blame, it also removes the feelings of accomplishment that accompany a job well done. Taking responsibility for small tasks can help the Indecisive Procrastinator feel that side of success.

Section Five Score: The Waiter

This person is waiting for someone else to step up to the plate and take charge. Ideally, her step-up person will complete a component of the project, give instructions, or help out a little. She often chooses people who won't be able to provide such assistance in order to avoid responsibility for the project. This person has often been blamed for things in the past.

- **Make forward motion.** The Waiter needs to overcome whatever fear she has about the future (whether it be failure, success, or the unknown) and see the benefit of forward motion.
- **Ask, why wait?** At the heart of this personality type is "a reason to wait." Waiting offers some benefit. It is important for the Waiter to ask herself what, precisely, she is waiting for. When she understands her reasoning, she can better create a supportive environment.

Section Six Score: The Control Seeker

This person is resistant to control by others or feels the need to be in control by choosing when and how things get done. (Often this control battle is not obvious but passive-aggressive.) Typically the Control Seeker is independent, resistant to instruction, and always seeking her own unique trail.

- **Tackle trust.** Trust is at the core of the Control Seeker's behavior. Controlling everything (or many things) prevents her from having to put faith in others. Often this person has had her trust broken many times and becomes a Control Seeker to avoid further hurt and disappointment.
- **Try teamwork.** While independence has its benefits, teamwork does too. Having at least one task or goal that is a "group project" can help the Control Seeker practice less controlling behavior.
- **Identify purpose.** The Control Seeker should ask herself what exactly she is trying to control. Often those who are controlling feel out of control in some area of their lives. This is then compensated for by becoming more controlling in another area.

Section Seven Score: The Needy Procrastinator
When we don't do certain things, sometimes someone else has to jump in and help. Procrastination can serve as a way to keep the Needy Procrastinator close to others through unhealthy dependence.

- **Overcome the fear of solitude.** The Needy Procrastinator may fear being alone based on previous experiences of rejection or abandonment. To compensate for this fear, she relies heavily on others. Recognizing that present behavior is triggered by past events is the first step in overcoming painful experiences.
- **Garner positive support.** The Needy Procrastinator needs to experience more positive interaction with others and recognize the joy that comes from contribution versus neediness.
- **Establish boundaries.** Adopting healthy emotional and physical boundaries encourages healthy communication with others.

Section Eight Score: The Overachiever
This person defines her self-worth by what she accomplishes. She takes on many tasks in hopes of validating her self-worth by completing them all. Often the number of tasks is unrealistic, and

in the end, she feels overwhelmed and paralyzed, which validates her negative self-worth and enables the cycle to continue.

Although similar to the Adrenaline Junkie, the Overachiever isn't necessarily motivated by the "rush." Instead, an Overachiever is motivated by status and accomplishments. This person defines her self-worth by what she gets done.

- **Ask, what am I proving?** Overachievers are typically trying to prove something to their immediate circle or the world at large. While accomplishing tasks is wonderful, when we push too hard, we eventually wear out. It is important to understand what we are trying to prove so we can find a healthier way of doing so.
- **Relax.** The Overachiever needs to learn how to sit still, relax, and let go.
- **Locate the source of self-worth.** She needs to learn that her self-worth will never be built by accomplishing tasks but by finding that quiet and grounded place within.

Section Nine Score: The Dreamer

The Dreamer has great ideas but lacks the skills (or direction) to create a realistic plan to reach her dreams; details go out the window.

- **Make solid plans.** The Dreamer needs to learn how to balance dreams with action and enlist the help of others to realize her dreams.
- **Focus.** The Dreamer often has many ideas or projects in the wings. Learning to focus and persevere with a given task or project is very important.

Section Ten Score: The Depressed Procrastinator

This personality type has tried many things and not achieved the desired results. She becomes depressed at the idea of a new task or project, predicting the outcome of the future will be the same as the past: unfulfilling.

- **Suspend disbelief.** The Depressed Procrastinator has to suspend her disbelief long enough to be hopeful that change can indeed happen.

- **Take small steps.** This person also needs to focus on the forward steps she takes, no matter how small, and quit focusing on what she doesn't do.

> **Exercise:** *After reading through the personalities, revisit column B of the Top Five worksheet. Next to each of the five items you wrote down, list which procrastination personalities were at work.*

My Prescription for Procrastination

Procrastination R_x

Today's date: _____

Project or task I am working on: _____

_____

Date prescription expires: _____

(This should be your completion date. For this mini-mission, choose something that can be completed between Monday and Friday of next week.)

In this particular area, I have discovered that my procrastination personality is _____

(Use the quiz to determine your personality type. If you ranked high in a couple of areas, you may list those.)

This personality type(s) has held me back by _____

_____

_____

_____

_____

This has hurt me in life by _____

_____

_____

_____

_____

By breaking this down into logical steps, I will complete the following:

Monday, I will _____

_____

Tuesday, I will _____

_____

Wednesday, I will _____

_____

Thursday, I will _____

_____

Friday, I will _____

_____

My reward come Friday will be: _____

_____

This is my prescription. Next week, I am willing to let go of the behavior that has held me back and create a new pattern. I understand this will be challenging, but by overcoming these challenges I will feel _____
and my life will improve because:_____

_____

_____

_____

Signature _____

Mark off each day that you complete your step:
__ Monday __ Tuesday __ Wednesday __ Thursday ___ Friday __

mini-makeover

overcoming magazine madness:
creating a personal reference library

"Out of clutter find simplicity."—*Albert Einstein*

In this Mini we look at how to transform magazines and other bound and printed matter from rarely consulted stacks to an efficient system by creating a Personal Reference Library.

Action Step Checklist

- ☐ Collect your content.
- ☐ Weed through time-sensitive and current material.
- ☐ Cancel any subscriptions (or transfer them) if you are not actively reading them.
- ☐ Create your reference categories.
- ☐ Set up your system.
- ☐ Build your binder.
- ☐ Finish your binder with a label.

For many people, paper clutter is one of the hardest piles to conquer. Every day more and more paper flows into our lives, and without a strategy to handle it, paper soon begins to pile up around us. Magazines are often the largest portion of the paper. While much of the content may be valuable, if it isn't organized, it becomes virtually impossible to efficiently find something when needed.

Think of your reference system as a collection of anthologies: instead of having everything grouped in one big pile, a well-kept reference system creates an effective system that groups like items together in three-ring binders. Imagine actually being able to find what you need—when you need it!

Step One: Collect Your Content

Gather all of your bound and printed matter, and place it into one of three categories:

1. Catalogs
2. Current-event magazines and time-sensitive materials
3. Reference (including manuals, non-time-sensitive magazines, trade publications)

This process is fairly quick and painless. Scan the magazine titles and divide them into these three categories. (If you have a lot of cooking magazines, you may want to make a fourth category for cooking- and recipe-related materials, and consider the Creating a Recipe Library Mini-Makeover in this book to help you sort your recipes.

What is a reference magazine/bound matter? "Reference" includes instructions, manuals, and any printed publication that you would need <u>in entirety</u> to make use of, such as magazines related to your vocation, directories, and the like. Some craft magazines also fall into this category, if you are a crafter *and* actually reference your magazines instead of letting them collect dust. The key to creating an effective reference system is this: <u>The material would actually be looked at numerous times if filed effectively</u>—*and* <u>would be valuable to look at.</u>

- **Example of non-reference:** I have an issue of a business magazine with a cover story on blogging that my husband gave to me. While the blogging article is one I want to read and may be an article I want to keep, the other articles are not; therefore the whole magazine is not reference and, for the sake of the next exercise, would <u>not</u> go in the reference magazine pile but in the "other content" pile.
- **Example of reference:** I subscribe to *Sommerset Studio* (a magazine of paper arts) and love it. I love browsing through any issue, any time, cover to cover for a break or for an idea. This would fall into reference.

Step Two: Weed Through the Time-Sensitive and Current Pile

When I did this exercise, one of our subscriptions was *People* magazine. I believe we had received it as a free promo on another purchase, as I do not remember subscribing. In any event, I am not an avid *People* reader. As I placed the *People* issues in the stack, I began laughing at the covers. One cover that caught my interest was a breakup of a famous couple. I began to browse the article during my sorting (a big no-no). I probably gave it about four to five minutes of my attention before setting it back on its stack.

Then the next issue reported they were back together. So I browsed that. Six issues later they were *really* separated. Three issues later they had worked it out—you get the idea. This type of publication rarely has long-term value, as the factual information it contains will most likely change.

The same is true of health-related publications. While the stories may be intriguing, rest assured they have discovered a new way to help you drop pounds or tone overnight. In addition, another doctor has more recently discovered the Five Most Amazing Energy Secrets. Remember how coffee has been good for us, bad for us, good for us, bad for us? <u>Keep only the current research and news—let the rest go. Cancel any subscriptions</u>

<u>you don't have time to read when "fresh"</u> — (Fresh is defined as within two issues of receipt. In other words if it is a weekly and you cannot read it before the next two issues arrive, let it go. For a monthly, if you cannot read it before the next two months arrive, let it go.) If you choose not to cancel it, place it in a "giveaway stack" and <u>give it to someone who will have time to read it</u> — Or better yet, make someone's day: give them to a friend by submitting a change of address request. Put your name on the top line and then c/o your friend's name on the next line along with her address. (You can often do this online if you have a copy of a subscription label handy.)

Tip for crafters and paper artists: *If you are a collage artist or use images in art, watch for catalogs (and magazines) printed on quality paper. You can put these into art-supply crates for inspiration and use in your art projects.*

Go through your magazines and see how many are no longer applicable or of interest. Is an old *Vogue* with fashions from the 1990s going to be something you consult today? If you are having difficulties, ask yourself this: *if I have thirty minutes of free, uninterrupted time, would I want to spend it reading this?*

If the answer is no, out it goes. If the answer is yes, place just the specific pages in a folder or envelope designated for "to-read" items. I take my to-read envelope with me to appointments and often find time to read through quite a bit while waiting.

Step Three: Work through Reference Magazines

Reference magazines are tricky because we often believe we might need them — hence the term "reference magazines." These magazines include just about any magazine that is not time sensitive. For example, the techniques in a stamping magazine will be just as cool in a year as they are now. Because there are so many reasons to keep everything, we need to raise our selection criteria so we are not overloaded.

> *Paper-Taming Strategy: Keep a separate binder for all instruction manuals. Then when you need to know how to use something, you can actually consult the manual—because you can find it! You can put software serial numbers in here too, if you tend to lose them. Make sure to prune once or twice a year to get rid of any paper pertaining to items you no longer have.*

- **Think logically about the system.** To build a reference library, you need to follow the basic guidelines of a library or bookstore: group by general topic. Examples might be arts and crafts, marketing, ancestry, reports, membership guides, travel, warranties.

    Take your reference pile and begin grouping it by topic, making sure to give warranties and instruction manuals their own pile. Depending on the amount of printed material you have collected, these could be big groups. If this is the case, when you are done, put them in boxes or plastic totes by topic so you can get them out of the way and work through the boxes thoroughly one at a time.

- **Decide what type of information you need.** On a sheet of loose-leaf paper write down "headers" for the major categories you believe you will reference: art, photography, graphic design, business, etc. Now create a list of subtopics within each category. Make sure to include only information that you honestly believe has at least a 60 percent or more chance of being referenced in the future.

These lists create a predetermined guide of the types of information we will reference. Without thinking through what we really need, we will keep too much.

The second reason we use subcategories is that using only major categories is ineffective for finding what you need when you need it. Imagine a book superstore having a business section or fiction section or craft section without any further groupings (such as romance, mystery, sci-fi, teen, literature).

Here is an example of subtopics included in my art category:
- Acrylic painting techniques
- Acrylic painting inspirations
- Watercolor painting techniques
- Watercolor painting inspirations
- Mixed-media painting techniques
- Mixed-media painting inspirations
- Pencil and colored pencil techniques and inspirations (I could break this down further but since I do not frequently use pencils and colored pencils, I will start with a broader category. The goal is to get organized "enough" — without getting over-organized)
- Card making (includes all card-making techniques — when I want to make a card, I don't decide what I am going to use first, so sorting by paper cards, stamped cards, etc., would not make sense for me)
- Collage and visual journaling techniques
- Collage and visual journaling inspirations (although collage and visual journaling are technically separate areas or magazines, the concepts and techniques can be used in both, so I keep them together)
- Cool gift ideas
- Cool decorating ideas
- Rubber-stamping projects (other than cards)

You will have different categories based on the type of information you seek. This list is provided only as a general example of how I created my categories.

Step Four: Set Up Your Binder
Place your category list in the inside pocket of your binder, or if using a view binder, place it on the front as a "cover" for the time being. Add tab dividers for your subcategories.

> *Tip: Start your binders with only the <u>main</u> category — in this example, that would be art. My tabs would be the subcategories. Like the cooking binder example given in Creating Your Recipe Binder Mini-Makeover, when the binder fills up, I move the largest category to its own binder. I then wait for it to fill up again before adding an additional binder.*

Step Five: Build Your Binder

Work through the topic you have chosen to start with, and rip out the pages that match the information you need for your reference library. Hole punch the page immediately and transfer it to the binder.

> *Tip: Often you will find that your article of interest is featured on one side of the page and a different topic covered on the back. I like to make an X over the back if this is the case. Then when I page through for ideas, I can automatically read an article through without the interruption of non-related material.*

Exceptions to the Rule

There are very few magazines for which this "exception rule" would apply, but since I have a magazine that falls under this rule, I wanted to share it with you. Occasionally there will be a gem of a publication in which 90 percent of the material is relevant to your interest. These magazines usually have very few ads — or the ads that they do have are informative or serve as inspiration. I love working with paper — collage and cards specifically — and am addicted to *Sommerset Studio*. Each month when it arrives, I dive into the pages and savor it like I would a Godiva truffle. Every page is an inspiration to me — in almost any area of art. While the magazine might show a stamped-paper project, I can see the layout being used in my acrylics or collage.

I keep every one of these issues in standing magazine sorters. I make sure to put them in this area right away instead of letting them drift into a pile. (I learned this the hard way, as I lost six issues and missed them so much I ordered back issues online!) While I have many other wonderful art magazines that I love to receive, 30 percent of the content is not relevant or is merely advertising. I only apply this rule to *Sommerset.* If you choose to apply this rule, keep the magazines grouped together in a standing magazine rack in your reference area. At the end of each year, I copy the table of contents from each issue and place it in a binder. This way, I can easily glance at the features and articles without having to pull out every issue. It ensures that I keep the system user friendly.

> *Tip: If you have some reference areas that are smaller, consider grouping them together in one binder. For example, I keep a few garden articles — but the collection is quite limited as my green thumb is limited. Likewise, I have some decorating ideas I have kept, but again, this is very limited, since I only have a few rooms I would consider redecorating. These categories can easily go into the same binder.*

Step Six: Label

Label your binders clearly on the spines! This will make it easier to find what you need at a quick glance.

Multitask and Make Someone's Day

When I work through this process, I often find some tidbit, article, or commentary a friend might enjoy. I have a "to-send" envelope nearby. When I come across such an item, I write a quick note to the person on the article — something short like, "Shelly — saw this and thought you might enjoy it. Thinking of you, Brook." I then tuck it in the to-send envelope. I have created a rule, though, for this envelope: it has to be emptied every thirty days and the contents actually <u>sent</u>; otherwise it becomes another pile. Over time, I found that most of my items were typically sent to one of six people. Once I had this roster of frequently used addresses, I made the system more efficient by putting prestamped, addressed envelopes in the large to-send envelope. This way, I could simply toss the information into the envelope and label, seal, and mail it the next day. I receive a lot of comments from the recipients about how they look forward to these little snippets. It is a great way to keep in touch with friends and family in the rush of everyday life.

mini-makeover

little time blocks

"Don't be fooled by the calendar. There are only as many days in the year as you make use of. One man gets only a week's value out of a year while another man gets a full year's value out of a week."—*Charles Richards*

"If only I could find the time" is an often heard lament of today's busy women. This might be better stated as "If only I could find the amount of time I <u>think</u> I need." Our days are filled with little time blocks that can be put to good use—if we are ready to take advantage of them. This Mini will show you how to maximize these unexpected time blocks.

Action Step Checklist

- ☐ Read the various ideas in this Mini.
- ☐ Create a list of any ideas that are useful to you, remembering to add your own, too!
- ☐ Keep this list handy to take advantage of unexpected breaks in the day.

Life Coach Sue Brenner, author of *The Naked Desk*, encourages people to maximize their time by brainstorming what can be achieved in small time increments: "To maximize your time, learn what you can do in small increments. It's not about cramming things in. It's about discovering brief openings of time in your day. What can you do with fifteen minutes? Don't fritter them away. Spend these small blocks of time intentionally on things that will make a difference." Additionally, breaking things down into doable components often releases us from "project paralysis." How many times have you thought, "I'll get to this when I have time"? Not surprisingly, the time never comes. However, with the focus of little time blocks, we can hone in on specific action steps. Most people are amazed at how much they can get done in a short, concentrated block of time.

Create a list of quick tasks and keep it in your planner. When a short break presents itself, you will be ready to take advantage of it.

Here are a few of Brenner's ideas:

- **Declutter your car.** Are you early for a meeting and want to get something done? Declutter your car! Gather up all the recyclables, including plastic bottles, soda cans, and paper, and put them in a bag. Put all trash in another bag. Use a damp cloth or disposable wipe to clean all surfaces. Group any remaining things that you need to remove from your car later, such as clothes and newly purchased items. When you leave your car, take all the trash and recycling with you. Remove the other items as soon as you get a chance. If you're picking up clients for a meeting, they'll appreciate the serene setting you've just created in your car.

Brook's Tip: I keep a travel-size pack of car wipes (or you can use household or even baby wipes) in my glove box along with a couple of dusting cloths. I also have a four-ounce, ninety-nine-cent plastic spray bottle filled with Windex. (You can find these spray bottles at stores like Wal-Mart, Walgreens, or Target.) This car kit takes up little room and allows me to take advantage of rush hour or an early arrival to an appointment by doing a quick clean. This kit has also come in quite handy when spills happen!

- **"Sprint clean" your office.** Scan your office. Pick the one area that needs the most attention first: Do you have folders stacked on your desk? Are there three coffee mugs from the past week? Your desktop may be your first target area for action. Remove what doesn't belong there. Use a tissue to dust. Either file papers or put them in your outbox for future organizing. The goal is to pick one area and clear it. Then experience a sense of calm and relief: eliminating a mess you've been putting up with recharges your batteries.

- **Fix something that is broken.** You know all those things you think to yourself: "I have to change the light bulb," "I need to get the latch on that window fixed," "I have to let IT know about my computer glitches"? Use a small time block to actually do something about them. If you're handy, take that time to actually fix something simple yourself. For example, if the arm of your chair dangles, find the screw and bolt under the seat, and tighten it up yourself. If you can't (or don't want to) fix something yourself, take the time to contact someone who can. Prompt your IT person to come assess your computer problems, or see if he or she can do it remotely. Call maintenance to repair your window. Take the first step so you can stop thinking about it.

- **Prep for a meal.** Do you find yourself eating out every day? Do you want to eat healthier but end up grabbing the quickest and most convenient food at meal times? When you have an extra fifteen minutes at night or in the morning, use it to prepare a meal. Slice some sourdough bread and make your favorite sandwich for a bag lunch. Then enjoy more time at noon because you won't have to run around and wait in line for your food. Your meal prep might include tossing some meat, spices, and vegetables into a slow-cooker or crock pot. Then you can return home from work to a nourishing, warm meal. You can sit down, relax, and enjoy your food solo or with your family.

For more of Sue Brenner's tips and tools, visit www.actionsymphony. com.

Ideas from Brook

- **Match the socks.** Grab a container and pile all solo socks inside. Match what you can.
- **Rotate the closet.** Do you really need all the winter coats in the coat closet during summer? If it is winter, is anyone going to wear the open-toed shoes? Move out-of-season items to an unused closet. If you don't have one, consider hanging a small line in an infrequently used area of the house. Once this is complete, look at what you have left. Are there items that "ended up" there but don't really need to be there? Move them to their proper home.
- **Repair "message central."** Wherever messages are taken, clutter seems to arise. Go through any miscellaneous messages or notepads and discard items no longer needed. Test the pens; get rid of those that don't work. Clear out your answering machine messages or voice mail.
- **Clean off the fridge.** While putting coupons on the fridge seems like a logical way to remind us to use them, it is amazing how quickly they age! Remove outdated items from your fridge display. If you have kids' artwork wallpapering the front, consider rotating artwork, showcasing an artist of the week.
- **Sort the mail.** Gather all the mail into one place. Don't read the mail; just make piles. Create a pile for garbage, one for bills, one for to-read items, and additional piles for other people in the home (i.e., mail for husband, child, mother). When done, transfer the piles for others to somewhere they will see them. Put the to-read items in a place you will read them. Toss the junk in the garbage. Return the bills to the inbox.
- **Go through the bills.** This is best to complete after the previous task. Remove all bills from their envelopes and lay them flat. Staple or paperclip those with multiple pages. Tuck the return envelope around the bill. Throw out all the miscellaneous offers included in the bills. Stack them in three piles: receipts/file only (if you use autopay), to pay within the next fourteen days, to pay after fourteen days.

- **Wipe down the appliances.** Grab the Windex and wipe down the front surfaces of your kitchen appliances.
- **Clear the junk drawer.** Empty the drawer entirely. Go through each item, and either throw it out or return it to its proper place. There is no reason to waste prime storage space on junk.
- **Sort your chargers.** If you are high tech, gather all of your gadget chargers together. Wrap the cords neatly. Label each one with its purpose. Move car-compatible chargers to the car. Place the others neatly in a drawer.
- **Wipe down the microwave.** Give your microwave a thorough cleaning—inside and out!
- **Wipe down a shower door.** Spray the front and back, and let it set for a couple of minutes while you wipe down the vanity area. Return and wipe down the shower door.
- **Wash a window.** Wash a set of inside windows (or outside, for that matter—your pick).
- **Match up your media.** Return CDs, DVDs, video games, and computer programs to their proper storage cases.
- **Go through your media.** Do you need to keep the install disks to printers you no longer own or programs you no longer use? Get rid of any items you don't need to make it easier to find what you do need.
- **Photograph your home.** Create a photo inventory of your home for insurance purposes.
- **Check the medicine cabinet.** Check the expiration date of all vitamins, prescriptions, and medicine-cabinet supplies, discarding any expired items.
- **Play the "bye-bye ten" game.** Find ten things in your house to donate or throw away.
- **Sweep the entry way.** Take a moment to sweep the outside entrance of your home.
- **Purge the Post-its.** Gather a stack of loose adhesive notes and transfer them to your planner.

Take Action

Use these ideas to begin building your own Little Time Block list.
Add your own ideas as well. Keep this list handy throughout the
day to maximize unexpected breaks.

mini-makeover

reality routines

"Building efficient, healthy, and rewarding Routines creates the foundation for building a life of contentment."—*Brook Noel*

In this Mini we work step by step through building a weekly Reality Routine. This is not a routine based on everything you <u>want</u> to do but based on the "anchors" that help you stay sane, maintain balance, and feel good about your home and self. By the end of this Mini, you will have created a solid routine and run it through the reality test.

Action Step Checklist
- ☐ Take inventory of home maintenance.
- ☐ Create a Life Maintenance Inventory.
- ☐ Conduct a Reality Check.
- ☐ Try out your routine.
- ☐ Evaluate and revise your plan as needed.

Often what we want to do and what we can actually find the time to do are in sharp contrast with one another. Best laid plans are lost when life goes haywire: the unexpected trip or unexpected guests, the overtime at work, the problem with a close family member, the unexpected illness, or the emotional roller coaster. During these times, a solid weekly routine is one tool that can help us keep our sanity and stay above the chaos. When life outside our homes is in disarray, the foundation of a solid routine within the four walls of home can serve as a touchstone of sanity.

To make a Reality Routine, we have to consider four types of information:

- **Home maintenance:** These are tasks done in the home. For example, I cannot clean my stove while I am at the grocery store.
- **Life maintenance:** These are tasks essential to keeping self and family functioning that require stepping outside your front door, like grocery shopping or dropping off and picking up dry-cleaning.
- **Commitments to self and others:** As the name implies, these are commitments we have made to ourselves or others. Examples include volunteering, meetings, and work requirements.
- **Anchors:** An anchor is an activity that feeds our energy and keeps us balanced in order to effectively achieve our Reality Routine.

Building Your Reality Routine
Step One: Take Inventory of Home Maintenance
It is best to begin in the most active area of your home, since this is where you spend the most time. For many people this will be the kitchen/dining area—often the "hub" of the home.

When completing this exercise, make sure to actually walk into the most active area and look around to make sure you don't miss anything.

If this area is in disarray, begin organizing and cleaning; however, only clean until you feel the "chaos feeling" lift. Then write down what you did. This is a good measure of how clean the area needs to be for you to be comfortable. If your area is already under control, write down the key components you need to do to keep it that way. Note the word need. This is not a time to list everything you want to do — just what you need to do to maintain a feeling of control and avoid the feeling of drowning in chaos.

Keep this list as short as possible. The goal is not perfection; the goal is to stay above the "chaos cutoff."

Here is an example of my need-to-do list from the kitchen:

- Empty and load dishwasher
- Wipe down counters
- Take out garbage
- Sweep
- Mop
- Wipe down dining room table (our kitchen and dining rooms are connected)
- Clear off surfaces (so I can get to them in order to wipe them down)

Remember, this is not about listing everything we would do in an ideal world; it is about doing what we **need** to do. A good way to test a need-to-do item is to ask, *why do I need to do it?* Carefully look at your answer to test the validity of the reason. For example, on my list, I need to empty and load the dishwasher because otherwise we would not have any dishes to use. I need to wipe down the counters because otherwise they would attract bacteria, germs, and ants.

Step Two: Walk into the Next Most Active Area and Repeat
I find that, in my family, about 8 percent of our living takes place in the kitchen, dining area, or family room. Therefore, in building my Reality Routine, my next stop would be the family room. Again, if the area is a mess I would begin cleaning only until I felt above the "chaos cutoff."

As I stand in my living room, I can quickly see the "need-to-do tasks are actually quite minimal:

- Round up loose items and return them to their proper home (a project I took out to work on, games my daughter and I played, a cup someone forgot to put away)
- Vacuum (since we often sit on the floor to play games)

Do you notice how short my need-to-do list is? Of course I could dust, wipe down the blinds, and find many other things to do in this room. However, when life is busy or interrupted, or when an emotionally draining time comes, <u>having a list a mile long with items like "wipe down blinds" and "dust knickknacks" is not what I need to focus on.</u> Instead, I need to focus on the reason life is busy, on the interruption, or on emotionally recharging.

Step Three: Walk through the Rest of Your Home and Identify Need-to-Do Tasks
For me, this list looks something like this:
- Change kitty litter
- Empty all garbage
- Water plants
- Do a pass to corral out-of-place items
- Do laundry
- Pay bills
- Open mail
- Vacuum/mop throughout home
- Change bedding
- Wipe down bathrooms

Again, if I compare this list to the list I use for a full clean, this list is much shorter. Why? Because it is the "base" upon which everything is built. If I complete this list <u>routinely</u>, then I feel in control, and my home maintains a level where I can invite anyone in at any time. Sure, it isn't perfect, but it is perfectly livable.

Step Four: Take Inventory of Life Maintenance
Life-maintenance tasks are actions and errands we must do in order to keep our lives and the lives of anyone with whom we live

functional. Remember, when working on your list, write down only those things that are routine — meaning they are repetitive tasks.

Here is a sample from my list:

- Grocery shop
- Stock up on bulk items once a month
- Prepare dinner
- Shower and get ready for the day
- Pack school lunch for my daughter
- Pack school bag for my daughter (sports uniform, etc.)
- Plan meals
- Drop off/pick up dry-cleaning
- Drop off/pick up prescriptions
- Go to bank

Step Five: Take Inventory of Commitments

Commitments are times we have committed to be present for an activity or complete an action — on a routine basis. Examples might include volunteer commitments, meetings, continuing education, workout classes, and clubs. You may also have variable or seasonal commitments. For example, right now I am teaching the Paper Piles and Files and High-Energy Living courses and helping on the Ten Weeks of Christmas course. However, in five weeks these commitments will be completed. I am going to list these all at the bottom so that in five weeks updating my Reality Routine is easy to do.

FAQ: Do I Include Work on This List?

If your work is heavily routine based, I would definitely add it to your worksheet. Personally, my work is built on routines — and a lot of them — that I need to maintain, or I would drown in the chaos of customer service. My work routines are actually a much longer list than my home routines, so I keep them on their own Reality Routine worksheet.

In the early 1990s, I worked as a waitress. That career did not require any routines except making sure I had a clean uniform and then being present. In the mid-1990s, I managed a six-hundred-unit apartment complex. That career had a few routines, but they all had efficient systems to manage on-site, and I had little influence in these automated routines. Again, my chief goal was to show up without a tear in my pantyhose. In

> *both of these instances, I would simply add "dry-cleaning" or "uniform*
> *prep" to my Reality Routine list and not break out specific actions.*

Step Six: Run a Reality Check

The goal is not to end up with the most tasks: the leaner this list, the better. Test each item on your list by making sure it needs to be done based on the test offered earlier: **This needs to be done because** _____.

To phrase it another way, *what would happen if this wasn't done?* If the task would take care of itself or there is little to no repercussion for not doing it, it may not need to be on your Reality Routine worksheet.

Remember, we will rely on this Reality Routine worksheet all the more in times of stress and craziness. The more concisely and carefully the tasks are chosen, the better. Think about the last time life threw you a curveball, and then look at your list. Would the list have been intimidating or doable? If the answer is intimidating, scale it back.

Step Seven: Add Anchors

Anchors are very important, yet often left off a woman's weekly schedule. An anchor is something we do (or would like to do) that can help us stay balanced and stay centered; we notice our life runs smoother when we do them.

These anchors are especially important when life gets busy or we are emotionally drained. But often, instead of upholding these anchors, women let them go to find time to meet other demands. I used to do this, too. Then I realized that without my anchors, my attitude and outlook took a turn for the worse, my energy was lower, and my self-esteem wavered.

Anchors are fuel for the body, mind, and soul. Without anchors we drift away from being balanced and find ourselves tired, irritable, short-tempered, negative, or overly sensitive to things we could once take in stride.

Your anchor list doesn't need to be long; it just needs to be *there*. A good way to identify your anchors is to ask, *when I look at times my life was "working," what was I doing that helped?*

For me, journaling, Bible study, an afternoon nap, living the Make Today Matter Toolbox, and working on my Minis are my key anchors. Other anchors I often hear are time out with my spouse, yoga, massage, walking, reading, sewing/needlecraft, scrapbooking, and meditation. This is far from an exhaustive list—just a few examples to get you started.

On the Reality Routine worksheet, list your anchors.

Step Eight: Add Frequency

Now that we have identified the components of a Reality Routine, it is time to figure out how often we will complete these tasks. The Reality Routine worksheet contains columns numbered one through seven and then a separate column for "other."

For each item, mark off how many days per week you will complete the task. For example, if you need to complete this action once a week, place a check mark in the one column. If you need to complete this item twice a week, place a check mark in the two column.

"Other" is for events that occur every other week or at a time you cannot factor into the seven-day formula. For example, "girls' night out" is part of my routine, but it is monthly, so I would write "second Thursday of the month" in the Other column.

Important: *In every category, excluding anchors, make sure this number reflects the <u>minimum</u> for keeping your home and life above chaos. You can always do it more often, if you choose to do so or have the time, but this is about a Reality Routine — the bare-bone basics.*

When it comes to frequency, anchors require a bit of experimentation. We want to schedule our anchors at a frequency that allows us to achieve the goal of sanity, self-refueling, and centeredness. I have one friend who finds that going to yoga once a week recharges her. I have another friend who needs to run at least three days a week to find stress relief.

Some people benefit from journaling once a week. While I can journal once a week, I find that daily journaling is what often keeps me sane and helps me process everything going on in my ever-racing mind. That said, if I did not place this on my list as a daily requirement, I probably wouldn't do it — at least not daily. Why, since I know how rewarding it is?

Anchors are often seen as self-indulgent, not as "sanity savers." When we face chaos or emotional drain, it can be hard to remember how important these sanity savers are. This is why we are putting them on the Reality Routine worksheet now: to make sure these important components are not forgotten.

Step Nine: Add Time
Using your frequency numbers, pencil in when each routine will become reality on the worksheet of your choice. Note that the bottom of each worksheet contains an area for "other." Use this to pencil in any actions or commitments that fell into your "other" category.

Step Ten: Live Your Routine
With everything in place, now it is time to live your routine and give it the true reality test. Check off each item or highlight it as you complete it.

Step Eleven: Evaluate and Revise
At the end of the week, ask yourself these questions:
- **Is there anything I did not get done?** If the answer is yes, then ask yourself if it truly needs to be on your Reality Routine worksheet and why to determine if it should stay or not.
- **Is there anything I did too much of?** In other words, did you schedule something to do five times per week, when really three times would suffice?
- **Did I complete my anchors?** If the answer is no, where will you move them to make sure you complete them?

Adjust your next Reality Routine based on your findings.

Step Twelve: Repeat, Reevaluate, Reach Reality
Continue to revise weekly until your Reality Routine is one that suits
you, <u>is reality</u>, and accomplishes the goals outlined in this Mini.

Reality Routine Worksheet

Reality Routine Worksheet								
Home Maintenance								
Description	1	2	3	4	5	6	7	Other
	1	2	3	4	5	6	7	
	1	2	3	4	5	6	7	
	1	2	3	4	5	6	7	
	1	2	3	4	5	6	7	
	1	2	3	4	5	6	7	
	1	2	3	4	5	6	7	
	1	2	3	4	5	6	7	
	1	2	3	4	5	6	7	
	1	2	3	4	5	6	7	
	1	2	3	4	5	6	7	
	1	2	3	4	5	6	7	
	1	2	3	4	5	6	7	
	1	2	3	4	5	6	7	
	1	2	3	4	5	6	7	
	1	2	3	4	5	6	7	
	1	2	3	4	5	6	7	
	1	2	3	4	5	6	7	
	1	2	3	4	5	6	7	
	1	2	3	4	5	6	7	
	1	2	3	4	5	6	7	
	1	2	3	4	5	6	7	
	1	2	3	4	5	6	7	
	1	2	3	4	5	6	7	
	1	2	3	4	5	6	7	
	1	2	3	4	5	6	7	
	1	2	3	4	5	6	7	

Continued...

Anchors								
	1	2	3	4	5	6	7	
	1	2	3	4	5	6	7	
	1	2	3	4	5	6	7	
	1	2	3	4	5	6	7	
	1	2	3	4	5	6	7	
	1	2	3	4	5	6	7	
Life Maintenance								
	1	2	3	4	5	6	7	
	1	2	3	4	5	6	7	
	1	2	3	4	5	6	7	
	1	2	3	4	5	6	7	
	1	2	3	4	5	6	7	
	1	2	3	4	5	6	7	
	1	2	3	4	5	6	7	
	1	2	3	4	5	6	7	
	1	2	3	4	5	6	7	
	1	2	3	4	5	6	7	
	1	2	3	4	5	6	7	
	1	2	3	4	5	6	7	
	1	2	3	4	5	6	7	
Commitments								
	1	2	3	4	5	6	7	
	1	2	3	4	5	6	7	
	1	2	3	4	5	6	7	
	1	2	3	4	5	6	7	
	1	2	3	4	5	6	7	
	1	2	3	4	5	6	7	
	1	2	3	4	5	6	7	
	1	2	3	4	5	6	7	
	1	2	3	4	5	6	7	
	1	2	3	4	5	6	7	
Work (if routine-based see Mini for instructions)								
	1	2	3	4	5	6	7	
	1	2	3	4	5	6	7	
	1	2	3	4	5	6	7	
	1	2	3	4	5	6	7	
	1	2	3	4	5	6	7	
	1	2	3	4	5	6	7	
	1	2	3	4	5	6	7	
	1	2	3	4	5	6	7	

Weekly Reality Routine Worksheet

Action	Mon.	Tue.	Wed.	Thu.	Fri.	Sat.	Sun.

self-time & self-discovery

"The name of the game is taking care of yourself, because you're going to live long enough to wish you had."—*Grace Mirabella*

To live life to the fullest, we need to take time to live. Inside the hustle and bustle, we need to carve out time to stay in touch with ourselves—to explore our goals and dreams and to nurture our body, mind, and soul. The Mini-Makeovers in this section offer simple ways to incorporate self-time and self-discovery into our busy days.

Mini-Makeovers
- Creating a Goal and Treasure Book
- Journaling toward Self-Discovery
- Journaling for Answers: Digging Deeper
- The Movie in Your Mind

mini-makeover

creating a goal and treasure book

"Visualize this thing that you want, see it, feel it, believe in it. Make your mental blue print, and begin to build."—*Robert Collier*

Thinking is often abstract. Because the human mind races, we can think about something without having a tangible and clear picture in our mind. Transforming thoughts to recorded words and images gives shape, definition, and substance to our intention.

Treasure Books involve creating a physical representation of what you want to achieve; they act as a constant reminder and representation of your goals. In turn, the process of creating (and reviewing) a Treasure Book acts on your subconscious mind to motivate and encourage you toward realizing these goals.

Action Step Checklist
- ☐ Choose your book format.
- ☐ Assemble your supplies.
- ☐ Complete the category-page assessment.

Many people think daydreaming is a useless exercise. They may be right, but I can guarantee that *visualization* is not a useless exercise. Visualization is the practice of vividly and clearly picturing something you wish to manifest in your life. The clearer this image is in your mind, the more likely the goal will materialize in reality. We must have a crystal-clear vision of what we want to bring into our life in order to find it.

A famous study compared two graduating classes. One of the classes wrote down where they wanted to be in five years, and the other class did not. When the researcher caught up with the two classes ten years later, an overwhelming 86 percent more of the people who had written down their goals had accomplished them. Adding visual images to written goals and intentions increases odds of realization even more.

A Treasure Book is a visual map, reviewed frequently to help you see what you want to create in your life.

Something happens when we commit our ideas to paper that science cannot fully explain. We set something in motion or visualize something in a new way, and it becomes a vital part of creating that reality for ourselves. Visualization itself is a very powerful technique. Many people find it challenging to create regular time to visualize or have a hard time visualizing what they would like to manifest. A Treasure Book offers a concrete and practical way to approach the important technique of visualization.

Choosing Your Treasure Book and Supply List

After I committed to creating my first Treasure Book, I was anxious to get started. Do you know what ultimately held me back? It may sound silly, but it was the process of choosing what to put my Treasure Book in. I could not make up my mind.

Altered books were just being introduced, and I was intrigued by the concept. (An altered book involves using an existing book— often an old book—and applying your words and images directly over the pages, occasionally letting some of the original page show through.) But I thought, "What if I add so much to my pages, I can't close the book?"

Next I considered using a scrapbook. Since there are a zillion to choose from, I was positive I could find one that "felt right." After browsing the aisles, I realized this felt too formal for me; it is important that whatever method you choose be welcoming and inviting. I was also concerned that I would quickly fill the scrapbooks and need a new one every two weeks! If this was going to become a regular practice, I would need an addition to store my scrapbooks and a large budget. Then I considered just using blank paper and stacking up the pages, but I worried that they would get lost or out of order and that this process was just too unstructured.

My System
Finally I chose a system that has worked well for me: I use sheets of 8½ -by-11-inch paper and a three-ring view binder. I create a Treasure page to insert in the front and back cover. Inside the binder, I place sheet protectors. This allows me to avoid hole punching the paper directly and keeps all the little "paper edges" in their spot. It also prevents the pages from sticking together. I can then put pages back-to-back by inserting two in a sleeve. If I add embellishments (such as beads, buttons, or a small pocket envelope), it ensures they will stay with their designated page. I can also easily update the book by changing and moving pages around.

If you prefer to work in a smaller format, you can create a similar system with a "photo brag book." These books are usually around four-by-six inches in size and can be found at bargain stores for a dollar or two. Stores like Target and Office Max typically carry them as well for around two dollars. You can then use four-by-six plain index cards for the pages. These are smaller and the number of pages is typically fixed, but if the format appeals to you, consider creating a series of themed Treasure Books.

Choose one of the four basic approaches that follow or create your own. If you cannot decide, sleep on it and choose tomorrow. If you still cannot decide, write them down on paper, throw them in a hat, and choose one. Trust your choice.

Supply Lists

Brook's System
You will need the following supplies:
- Three-ring binder (a view binder is great). See if you have any on hand.
- 8½-by-11-inch paper, preferably card stock. Your best bet for this is an office-supply store versus a craft store. Office-supply stores sell letter-sized card stock that is archival in quantities of 250 sheets for around six to twelve dollars.
- Page protectors

Altered Book
Any book you choose and any size you like will work fine. This can be an old book, a new book, or an unread book. If you don't have a book on hand (which I doubt, if you look high and low), try the bargain bin of your local bookstore or an online bargain bin. Choose a book that has words or images that are appealing to you. Work right over the pages.

Scrapbook
For some people, a scrapbook will be the best fit. Choose any color/style you like. If you have one around the house, all the better.

Brag Book
Use a four-by-six-inch brag-book format and index cards as the "card stock."

Other Supplies
You can make this process as creative or as simple as you choose. At minimum you will need the following:
- Glue stick or other adhesive
- Magazines you can cut up
- Scissors
- Envelope or page protector to store images you have cut out or other paper (you may want to have several on hand, one for each themed page you are working on)

- Pen or marker
- Crayons, paints, colored pencils (optional)

Book Block

The first page you make can be intimidating—especially if you think you're not creative. Creativity doesn't matter. The goal of a Treasure Book is not to create an artistic masterpiece but to offer concrete images of your intentions. If you experience "book block," set a timer for twenty minutes and force the process of making a page. While I realize that doesn't sound very relaxing, it breaks the ice. Continue in this fashion until you get comfortable approaching the blank page.

Book Building

While reading this Mini will help you understand the importance of a Treasure Book, it is up to you to take action and bring the exercises to life. Schedule a regular time to work on your Treasure Book. A good goal is at least one Treasure session a week.

Project: Category Treasure Pages

- **Step One:** The following list includes the major categories from the Snapshot used in the *Change Your Life Challenge* program (CYLC). If you are familiar with CYLC and use the Snapshot Tool, use your current Snapshot to prioritize the Life Areas. If you are not familiar with CYLC, number these areas sequentially, using a one to indicate the area <u>most</u> in need of your attention. Continue numbering through thirteen, using the number two to denote the second area most in need of attention, etc.

  _____ Work
  _____ Community
  _____ Spirituality
  _____ Family
  _____ Self-Time
  _____ Health and Energy
  _____ Home (peaceful home/home maintenance)

_____ Time Management
_____ Relationship
_____ Friends
_____ Health
_____ Finances
_____ Attitude, Outlook, Self-Esteem

Each of these categories could be a page in your Treasure Book. You do not need to fill all the pages right away; instead focus on the category most needing attention. Typically, I use a sheet protector for each themed page I am working on and just tuck images inside as I find them until I am ready to focus on the page. Alternatively you could create an envelope for each theme and add images as you find them.

- **Step Two:** Find the area you labeled with a "one," and begin with that topic for this exercise. Create a clear, general statement about what you want to achieve in this area. You might have a single goal, or you might have a collection of desires to manifest in this Life Area.
  - **Example 1:** I want to incorporate more self-time and creativity in my life to increase balance.
  - **Example 2:** I want to create a more peaceful and well-balanced home.

Brainstorm at least three specific actions that support your statement and list them below it.

Here are some actions for the first example, "I want to incorporate more self-time and creativity in my life to increase balance":

- Begin my day with a short journal entry
- Make a weekly "date" to paint or collage
- Surround myself with inspirational and eye-pleasing images
- Connect with others who have a passion for the creative process

Here are some actions for the second example, "I want to create a more peaceful and well-balanced home":

- Maintain a weekly maintenance schedule that keeps our home clean and welcoming

- Scale back and simplify collections to create more open space
- Explore do-it-yourself projects that allow cost-effective ways to add color and style
- **Step Three:** Begin paging through magazines and cutting or ripping out images that represent your general statement and your specific actions. They do not have to be specific pictures — such as a person sitting at a table journaling — but just visual representations that work for you. The world does not need to know what this Treasure Book means — only you do.

Tip: Keep an eye out for words or phrases that express the area you are working with. You may also want to add quotes. There are many great quotes at www.quotegarden.com on a variety of topics. You can handwrite your quotes directly onto your page or type and print them in your favorite font on your computer.

- **Step Four:** Once you are pleased with your collection, arrange these images on the page in a composition that is satisfying to you, and then affix them to the page. If you find perfectionism is a problem, give yourself a time limit. It is more important to complete the page than it is to create a masterpiece.
- **Step Five:** At least every other day, glance through your Treasure Book and visualize your goal. Place your book somewhere you will remember to glance at it.

About My Page

I have included a sample of the page I created for the home category.

First, you might note there aren't any straight edges. I always joke that I "failed scissors." Actually, I don't have the patience to use scissors, as I can never find a left-handed pair in this house. I simply rip my images by hand and layer them. I have always loved the way this looks and the "freedom" it brings to the process. If you haven't ever tried it, I encourage you to do so!

I chose several images with light and fun colors. I love the feeling of the clean and uncluttered home (and have a bit of uncluttering to do after a recent office move). For this reason, I looked for images that felt spacious to me. Next, I added some words that I had stumbled across while looking for home images. The top left image says "Take a productive break" (something I often need to remind myself to do).

The three circles in the image are cut from one of my art prints, reminding me to incorporate my love of art into my home. The card is from a deck of cards and represents playing games with my daughter — one of my favorite activities in the world.

All in all, the page reminds me of the joy, peace, and possibility that can be found when our home and relationships are in order — and the importance of maintaining a system and lifestyle that allows these priorities to shine.

mini-makeover

journaling toward self-discovery

"In this place without borders, new worlds can be created."—*Marlene A. Schiwy*, A Voice of Her Own

- Have you ever had the sense that you need to "discover" something—but you were unsure of what?
- Have you ever felt that an experience must have something to teach you but been unable to uncover the lesson?
- Have you ever wondered why you think the way you do, act the way you do, or make the decisions that you make?
- Have you ever wondered how your past shapes your present?
- Have you ever suppressed emotions and feelings to the point that you feel they are "eating you up inside" and you need to get them out?
- Have you ever wanted to record a memory in vivid detail so you could cherish it always?
- Have you ever felt like your life was on autopilot and you just wanted to slow down?
- Have you ever just needed a companion that you can truly open up to—without fear or boundaries?

These are just some of the needs journaling can help us fulfill. When I lived in the Pacific Northwest, I taught a journaling class at the University of Washington–Vancouver. I saw the transformations that occurred as both men and women unraveled life's mysteries on paper. It is some of this material that I will share in this Mini-Makeover.

Action Step Checklist

☐   Complete your first freewrite.
☐   Collect your journaling supplies.
☐   Commit your journaling routine to paper.

About seven years ago I was helping my mother clean out her home, the home where I had been raised until I moved on to create a home of my own. I discovered a box filled with journals I had maintained throughout the years. I carefully looked through the aged papers in search of my earliest journal entry. I found one that dated back to 1977, when I was four years old.

I was in preschool and the entry was in poem form, titled, "All About Combs." The ode that was likely written to be moving at age four brought a smile to my face. I had written at length about the pains of not having a comb on picture day. Apparently my long hair had chosen to become "frizzy" and many of the other kids had combs to "freshen up" pre-photo, whereas I did not. From the emotion-filled entry, I am guessing this was a fairly traumatic event.

Journaling has continued to be a companion throughout my life. I have used journaling to define myself, increase self-awareness, work through problems, and discover potential.

Journaling Technique: Freewrite

I believe freewriting is the most creative and successful journaling technique for self-discovery. I have seen this technique perform wonders in my own life and the lives of my students. If you are not familiar with freewriting, the first time you read the instructions you might wonder, *how will that be useful?* Don't worry. Just do the exercises, and I think you will soon discover the benefit!

Read the following instructions in their entirety and then conduct your first freewrite.

1. Find ten minutes where you won't be interrupted (or tell everyone to leave you alone for ten minutes!).
2. Find a digital watch, clock, or timer. If you're near a computer, go to www.online-stopwatch.com for an easy-to-use timer.
3. Have several pieces of paper and a pen together.
4. Take a few deep breaths.

5.   Set the timer or watch the clock for the next minute to come. When it does…

6.   Write and write and write and write and write some more… and when you write, follow these rules:

   - Do not erase anything or cross anything out.
   - Do not stop writing for any reason. If you can't think of anything to write, then write that—*I can't think of anything to write, I can't think of anything to write*—over and over again.
   - Do not judge what you are writing; just write.
   - Do not worry about grammar or word choice.
   - Do not let your pen stop putting ink on paper until the timer goes off.
   - Choose one of the following writing prompts to begin your entry. When you find yourself out of things to write, begin again with the same journal prompt.

Freewriting Prompts

   - I feel…
   - I like…
   - I need…
   - I think…
   - I remember when…

   - I want…
   - I hope…
   - I believe…
   - If I could…
   - I wish…

Activity One
Go ahead and complete your first freewrite; your creative adventure has begun.

Journaling Technicalities

My guess is that some of you were surprised and apprehensive that we jumped in to journaling without a lot of preamble. You might have been wondering, *Should I type this or write this? I only have this type of paper handy — is that okay?* Don't worry; I am going to back up today and cover all the technical questions I often hear. Having a sense of order and organization is important in the process, but it is only a tool in the process.

In activity one, I wanted to clearly demonstrate that journaling doesn't have any hard-and-fast rules. Journaling is about uncovering what is already there. We don't need a specific pen or piece of paper to do that. All we need is time. Often when we wait to start something, apprehension can build up and stop us before we begin. By diving in, you survived that "cold plunge into warm water." Now putting the tools in place will make the water more inviting.

Computerized or Handwritten Journals
Whether you choose a computer or notebook is a matter of personal preference. Most of us have a natural preference between typing or handwriting for creative work. At one point, it was believed that writing (as opposed to typing) increased the creative flow. I believe that these studies have more to do with personal comfort level. If we are not comfortable on a computer and/or it carries a lot of distractions (email, instant messages) or negative connotations (work), then it isn't a good creative choice. For others, the thought of writing longhand might bring back memories of torturous papers from school years. In this case, a computer might be just the ticket.

I personally do a bit of both. I keep a small journal with me at all times for taking notes or impromptu entries. (The journal I have for this is an inexpensive four-by-six-inch spiral notebook that I bought at Target for forty-nine cents.) I do the rest of my journaling on my laptop, unless I feel like using colored pens, pencils, or markers.

Things to Consider
- **Portability:** A paper notebook is more portable than any other source. If you do not have a laptop, I would strongly recommend a handwritten journal, as you will likely want your journal to be a constant companion. Even if you do have a laptop, a handwritten journal offers some benefits. For example, you might look silly (or be uncomfortable) curling up in your bed to do some evening reflection on your laptop; curling up with a notebook may be more enticing.
- **Added Meaning:** If you are new to journaling, I recommend a handwritten journal. Our writing itself (hard/soft, big/

little) can relay quite a bit of meaning when we look back on our entries. In addition, you may want to use different colors for different moods or topics as you progress.

- **No Deletion:** As you learned in activity one, deleting/erasing/crossing out is not an option if you desire the best results. If you think you will be tempted by the backspace/delete key, then the computer is not a tool for you.
- **Privacy:** 100 percent privacy is a must for the journal writing experience. We must be comfortable in the knowledge that our journal is for our eyes only (unless we choose to share an entry). It is easy to protect a computer file with a password or to keep a free private journal online at an encrypted, secure site such as www.livejournal.com. If you choose to keep a handwritten journal, find a secure physical place to keep it, carry it with you at all times, or invest in a small fireproof safe (which is what I did when I used a handwritten journal).
- **Longevity:** Computer users—make sure to back up your files regularly. If you password protect your file, make sure to write the password somewhere. Put it in a recipe book or a written address book. One time I had a two-hundred-page computer journal and protected it with one of my long-winded, nonsensical passwords. A few years later, I wanted to go back and reread some of my entries on that disc. I couldn't (and still haven't) found the password! Pen and paper users—consider a fireproof safe to keep your journal safe from fire, flooding, etc.

Supply List for Pen and Paper Journals
- **The Journal Itself:** Some people like to go out and purchase a really nice and more expensive journal. For those comfortable with that, great. I personally had a hard time purchasing more expensive journals when I started on my endeavor. Since I had paid a higher price, I was scared of "making a mistake." Instead of feeling inviting, it felt intimidating. I settled on spiral-bound journals with colored paper. They are only a couple of dollars each and feel good to me: not too large so

I can work with it anywhere. What feels good and inviting should be your guiding principle when purchasing a journal. Flip through the pages, imagine writing in it, and follow your instinct. Lined or unlined is simply a matter of preference.

- **Pens:** Pick up a nice package of pens that you would enjoy writing with, perhaps multiple colors for different moods. (Always pick pens, not pencils; with pencils, it can be tempting to erase.) I like to work with Pilot brand pens and purchase a pack of six. I use different colors for different types of entries or for Mind Mapping (a technique we covered in a previous Mini-Makeover).

Think about what type of journal you will keep, and set time aside to pick one up this week. You can always tape or glue in your other entries once you decide on your journal.

When to Journal

When I am teaching my health classes, I am often asked the best time to exercise. I often respond jokingly, "Whenever you are the most likely to do it!" While science shows exercise is best in the morning, if a particular person refuses to exercise in the morning, then morning obviously isn't best for that particular person.

Each of us is unique. Each of us processes thoughts, images, and events in a unique way. Understanding how journaling times can benefit your creative process allows you to better use this tool on the road to self-discovery.

Many people find that writing in the morning allows them to start "fresh and clean" for the day. The drifting thoughts, preoccupations, and distractions melt on to their morning pages, allowing them clear focus and more energy for the day.

Other people like to write before they go to sleep in order to release any tensions of the day, work through problems while they are still fresh on their mind, and record any lessons of the day.

There isn't a right or wrong way; there is only "your way," waiting to be discovered.

Your Journaling Space

Anything worth attaining involves a process. An athlete, doctor, or lawyer isn't born overnight. Study, experience, and practice are required to take someone from the starting point to where they want to be.

Journaling is no different. Those who journal regularly will realize results on a daily level over time. Those who journal weekly will likely realize weekly results. If you journal once a year, you will likely gain a bit of insight but nothing compared to the insight and wisdom that can be gained through more regular practice.

How often do you need to journal to see results? That varies person to person. I have found that journaling at least four to five times a week is the pattern I need in my life. Others must journal daily, others less. The only way to learn what works best for you is through exploration.

Considerations for Regular Journaling

- **Find a quiet time.** Consider your schedule and where you can find ten to twenty minutes of uninterrupted time.
- **Keep everything together.** Keep all of your journaling supplies together (pens/colored pencils/discs/etc.) in one box. Make a place for that box, and always return it to the same place. Otherwise, you will likely spend ten to twenty minutes trying to find your journal, a working pen, etc.
- **Find a comfortable place.** Choose a space that you find inviting (or several places). Perhaps it is outside, at a park or café, curled up on the couch, or in a favorite room of the house. Choose spaces conducive to creativity. Writing in the middle of a messy room or next to a stack of bills will not help you tap into the "right brain."

Activity Two

Take a moment now to commit your journaling schedule to paper. You are worth it. Write down when and where you will journal for the month. Keep this appointment just as you would any other appointment. After all, a missed journaling appointment could be a missed life discovery!

mini-makeover

journaling for answers:
digging deeper

"In this place without borders, new worlds can be created."
—*Marlene Schiwy*

In the protected pages of journals, we don't have to worry about what other people might think. We don't have to justify why we think or feel the way we do. We don't have to have the answer. We don't have to live up to anyone's expectations. In this space we need not rely on the mind but get in tune with—and rely on—the heart. This private space is not primarily concerned with what others need from us but what we need from ourselves. In this Mini we dig deeper into the self-discovery process afforded by the written word.

Action Step Checklist
- ☐ Complete the Reflections exercise.
- ☐ Complete the Following Freewrite activity.
- ☐ Begin building your idea bank.
- ☐ Complete the A Woman Speaks activity.

In order to understand why journaling is so effective, it helps to understand some basics about how the mind works.

Our minds use linear thought processes. We connect point A to point B to point C. We make decisions based on knowledge of what we have learned in the past. We assess a situation by taking the knowledge we have from the past, the expectations of those around us, and our perceived outcome. We combine this together and make the most logical choice we are able to make at the time with whatever circumstances, events, and decisions we are presented with. These are linear thought processes.

If we weren't able to do these things, we would not be able to care for ourselves or others or even balance a checkbook, because we wouldn't embrace cause and effect. The ability to be logical, sequential, and objective is the basis for human survival, and it occurs in the left hemisphere of the brain.

A quick illustration of the left and right brain hemispheres might look like this:

Left Brain	Right Brain
Logical	Random
Sequential	Intuitive
Rational	Synthesizing
Analytical	Subjective
Objective	Looks at the whole
Looks at parts	

While we are living in this left side, we often suppress anything that doesn't fit the "left mold." We suppress the illogical, the senseless, the "crazy idea," the impulse, the coincidence, and the big picture. As we suppress these notions, we lose touch with them.

However, if we *only* use this type of left-side linear thinking, we greatly limit our ability to discover new things and new solutions. Studies show that many of the processes involved in thinking "outside the box," brainstorming, arriving at new ideas or solutions, and understanding are located in the right hemisphere. The right hemisphere is creative and random; it doesn't care for logic or sequence.

Our everyday life calls for the left hemisphere to dominate in order for us to function. When we dial a phone number, it is the left side that puts the number into a logical sequence. The right side would just push some numbers at random to see what might happen. The left side holds on and predicts the answer; the right side lets go and lives the answer. When we use just one, we have one-sided thinking. When we combine the two, our life becomes a rich journey.

To let the right side "speak," we need to give it room and take away the left side's rules. Freewriting does just that. Freewriting isn't concerned with outcome, logic, sequence, or rules. Freewriting is simply about writing. It's like working a muscle; the more we freewrite, the more we exercise the right side, and its ability to express these insights and discoveries grows stronger.

Reflections

Tonight, sometime after dinner, allow room for your creative time. Spend ten to twenty minutes journaling, filling the designated space with a freewriting response that uses one of the following prompts:

- Today I…
- Today I learned…

Following a Freewrite

In this next activity, I want to show you how freewriting can be the first thread in a path of exploration. Gather the freewrites you have done thus far. Reread them, being careful not to pass judgment. Look for a sentence that surprises you, resonates with you, or leaves you feeling a strong emotion. Read through both entries in their entirety, and mark any sentences that meet those criteria. (Note: If you say that none of the sentences meet those criteria, then you are either being too hard on yourself or you didn't write for the full ten minutes. Go back and look again.)

Out of the sentences that you have marked, choose one of the sentences to work with today and write or type it at the top of your journal page.

Do a ten minute freewrite using this sentence as your starting point. Here are a few prompts:

- When I read this I think…
- When I read this I feel….

- This sentence makes me want...
- Another thing I could say about this is...

Building an Idea Bank

Building an idea bank ensures you never start a blank page wondering, *what should I write?* While the freewrite technique can be used to overcome any blank page, sometimes it is fun to have guided direction.

- **Random Idea Bank:** To create a random idea bank, you can use small scraps of paper cut into strips to record your journal prompts and then choose one randomly.
- **Themed Idea Bank:** To create a themed idea bank, use a small spiral notebook or index cards. If using index cards, color code cards by theme (one color per theme). If using a notebook, label each page with a theme. What are themes? Themes are the categories you give to the journaling prompts you find; for example, you could write out a list of values and use the values as prompts. Or you could write out a list of people to journal about, or a list of years, states, vacations, tough questions, memories — the sky is the limit!

Take These Ideas to the Bank...the Idea Bank
Use the following ideas to begin building your own idea bank:

- Use the prompts given in activities that you did not use for your freewrite.
- Experiment with "timed" freewrites. Try a five-minute timed writing and a ten-minute timed writing.
- Use the journal prompt "I wish..." for a two-minute freewrite. At the end of two minutes, choose any word you used in the freewrite and do a two-minute freewrite on that word. Continue this process until you have done five freewrites of two minutes each.

Activity: Build a themed or random idea bank using the prompts in this Mini for inspirations. Add ten of your own prompts as well!

- "I remember when…"
- "One of the happiest times of my life was…"
- "I knew I was in trouble when…"
- Create a list of ten things you want to remember about today (this week, this month—any other time period will do).
- Write about a childhood event. Try writing it in the first person, as if you were still that age.
- Freewrite about an unanswered prayer that turned out to be a blessing in disguise.
- Write down ten lessons you have learned in life. Aim to add a new lesson to this list every month.
- Write a letter to someone you need to forgive, but don't send it.
- Write a letter to someone you need to apologize to. Consider sending it.
- Write a conversation that has never occurred but would help you if it did.
- Choose a favorite story or movie and rewrite the ending.
- Choose a favorite story or movie and rewrite the beginning.
- Grab a novel at random (that you haven't read yet) and open to any paragraph. Write down the paragraph and then continue writing what would come next.
- Take your journal to a public place, such as a café. Choose someone at the café and freewrite about what you think that person's life is like or how the dialogue might play out if you spoke.
- Become a "noun": think of your favorite city or place to visit, and freewrite a journal entry as if that place could talk.
- Start an entry with "If these walls could talk…" See where it leads you.
- Time travel to other years and imagine what your life would be like. For instance, how would your life be different if you were alive in early 1900 versus now? What would have to do without? How would that improve or hinder your life?
- Turn on the radio to a station where you can understand the lyrics (not the stuff my daughter listens to these days!).

Write down the first lyric you hear, and use that as a basis for the journaling technique of your choice.

- Open a book at random and take the first sentence you read. Use that as a basis for the journaling technique of your choice.

- Find a CD you like. Listen to several songs and journal while you listen, writing about anything the music makes you feel or inspires you to write about.

- This last prompt might seem funny — and it usually starts off as such — but it can end up truly revealing a lot! Use a journaling technique of your choice (I like to use the freewrite) to explore this statement: "The things I have in common with a ____ are..."

A Woman Speaks

Anais Nin is one of the world's most renowned journal keepers. In the book *A Woman Speaks* she shares this reader Q&A.

Reader: I'm not presently keeping a diary, but sometimes I do feel the need to sit down and write down my feelings. So I decide I will write a diary; I get everything ready, open the book, and then comes the question: where do I start?

Nin: Put yourself right in the present. This was my principle when I wrote the diary — to write the thing I felt most strongly about that day. Start there and that starts the whole unraveling, because that has roots in the past and it has branches into the future.

Activity: Complete another freewrite using one of the three following prompts:
- Today, I feel most strongly about...
- Today, I want to remember...
- Today, my mind is preoccupied by...

Continue journaling regularly to gain deeper understanding into your life patterns. Several times a year, take a "quiet day" to review and reflect on the words you have written and realize what they reveal about your life journey.

mini-makeover

the movie in your mind

"Watch your thoughts…they become your words. Watch your words… they become your actions. Watch your actions…they become your habits. Watch your habits…they become your character. Watch your character…it becomes your destiny." —*Frank Outlaw*

Did you know that the story of your life creates a movie in your mind? The movie you have created thus far goes with you everywhere. Understanding this metaphorical movie offers insight into why we act or respond in the ways we do. Once we are aware of our personal movie, we can also act as the director and edit it in ways to better our lives.

Action Step Checklist
☐   Complete Reflection Question #1.
☐   Complete Reflection Question #2.
☐   Complete Reflection Question #3.
☐   Complete Reflection Question #4.
☐   Complete Reflection Question #5.
☐   Complete Reflection Question #6.
☐   Complete Reflection Question #7.

Understanding this concept can help us learn a lot about ourselves and about our interactions with others. Differences of opinion and disagreements are easy to explain, given we are all operating from our unique experiences.

Just as television screens have controls like "brightness" and "contrast," our screen has controls. Our beliefs, emotional state, physical energy, needs, history, and genetic disposition act as controls. Each control can fluctuate, creating many different ways our moments can be viewed. Reflect for a moment about how fatigue can influence your physical capability and emotional responses. This is just one example of a "control" that we have the power to influence.

What You Need to Know about the Movie in Your Mind

Reality? Many of us think we are seeing reality. We are actually only seeing our own personal reality. Our movie, our experience, will sway what we see. We experience reality by what is playing in our mind. That is why it is so important to be aware of what you feed into your mind to begin with.

It is impossible to be 100 percent objective. One person asked me, "What about scientists? They deal with facts—which must be reality-based, right?" While a scientist's job is to uncover, analyze, and use facts, the process is still objective and influenced by the mind. Take Claudius Ptolemy, for example. He was convinced the sun was rotating around the earth. Or how about when scientists believed the world was flat? The one fact we do know is that we are each influenced by our beliefs and experiences and therefore cannot truly see a given experience in the exact same way as another person. This is not a fault, just a fact.

The Voice-Over

All of your thoughts become part of your internal movie. These thoughts become the voice-over. We all know that in a real movie, the narrating comments have the ability to make or break a flick. The same is true with the commentary you add to your movie.

Reflection Question #1: What have you been thinking primarily over the past week? What type of movie would your thoughts

create? A drama? Comedy? Action flick? Romance? Horror? Is it a
movie you would want to see? Is it a movie you would want to star
in? Record your reflections here.

_____

_____

_____

_____

_____

_____

_____

Television Tune-Up

Just as you can take in a real television and have the controls adjusted,
you can adjust your controls. Positive materials, classes, and group
support are all mechanisms for fine-tuning your programming. On
the flipside, hanging out with negative people and engaging in self-
destructive habits and poor self-talk will distort your screen.

Reflection Question #2: What are five positive actions you can
take to tune your movie for the better?

_____

_____

_____

_____

_____

_____

Reflection Question #3: What are five habits or activities that
negatively influence your programming? What steps can you take
to cancel them?

_____

_____

_____

_____

_____

_____

No TiVo Required

While we might need a VCR or television to record our favorite programming, the mind has its own TiVo. It records, catalogs, and collects your experiences. When you face a new experience, it goes into the archives and finds related experiences. This is often all done at a subconscious level. This is why awareness and "fact checking" are so important. Before we make important decisions on "autopilot," it is a good practice to check the information we are basing our decisions on. Often the information may be outdated. It might be relevant in the past, but given our development, the old data may no longer be applicable.

For example, we may have learned certain behaviors or "rules" from our parents or society that we accepted as given facts, such as, "A house needs to be kept clean at all times" or "Always put all extra money in the bank." Perhaps these are rules you want to maintain in your reality—but maybe they are not. Maybe you have outgrown them.

Reflection Question #4: Are there any "given facts" that you may need to reprogram? Sometimes it is helpful to think through what we have learned by area: What beliefs did you learn about money? Health? Time? Work? Child rearing? Attitude? Self-identity? Self-care? Maintaining a home? Family? Relationships?

_____

_____

_____

_____

_____

_____

_____

_____

_____

_____

_____

Know What Is Playing

We need to be careful of what "scene" is playing when we are communicating with others. Often a person may come to us with an idea or brainstorm, and we play a past "criticism script" and interpret the information in a negative way. Becoming aware of what messages are playing can help us "hear" what people are actually saying more objectively.

For example, let's say at my last job I was used to a manager who seemed to constantly be looking for flaws or pointing out mistakes. Now, in a new job, my manager comes and asks me why I used Word to create a specific report instead of another program. This could be a completely innocent question, or maybe she liked the results better and wants to switch! However, if I am not careful I might interpret this as a negative question based on my past experience.

Reflection Question #5: Over the course of the week, listen to what "script" is playing when communicating with others. Make some notes about how this awareness altered your response.

Influences

Your emotional and physical state affect what you see. Have you ever noticed that some days a to-do list will seem absolutely impossible and overwhelming, whereas other days that same list seems like a piece of cake? How we feel both emotionally and physically dramatically affects the screen of our mind. Have you ever seen a television show where the audio track doesn't line up with the picture? The person is speaking, but the words don't match his or her mouth movement. This is what happens in our minds when we are tired and overextended: we keep talking, but it doesn't "match up." If we want our minds to give us a solid base for living and loving life, we have to maintain self-care that keeps us emotionally and physically strong.

Reflection Question #6: What self-care helps you maintain your best physical and emotional energy?

Lights, Camera, Action

Now that you are aware of the movie in your mind, know that you are also the sole producer and director with the ability to edit your movie. You can change the voice-over commentary and add new experiences to take control of the script.

Reflection Question #7: This week be aware of the movie in your mind. When you are happy, take a moment to think about what is "playing." When you find yourself upset or distressed, what's on the screen? Are there any outdated scenes you need to permanently archive? What voice-over commentary and new experiences can you add to take control of your script?

attitude & self-esteem

"Attitudes are contagious. Are yours worth catching?"—*Dennis and Wendy Mannering*

While this is the last section, it is certainly not the least. Attitude and self-esteem are the seeds from which everything else grows. Have a good attitude, and you will set yourself up for good. Have a bad attitude, and you will set yourself up for bad. The Minis in this section will help you keep a good attitude in check or transform a bad attitude into a positive, productive one.

Mini-Makeovers
- Staying Centered
- Recapturing Daily Magic Part One: Back to Basics
- Recapturing Daily Magic Part Two: Beyond Ourselves
- Facing Fear and Stepping outside the Comfort Zone

mini-makeover

staying centered

"When we can't access our inner resources, we come to the flawed conclusion that happiness and fulfillment come only from external events."—*Sarah Ban Breathnach*, Simple Abundance

Have you ever noticed how once you start worrying about something or dwelling on something, it can be hard to stop? Before we know it, we have spent hours analyzing, thinking about, worrying over, or discussing something we are not pleased about. All of this time increases gloom and negativity—and it is time we cannot get back. Learning how to stay centered can help us avoid the negative spiral and make healthy choices.

Action Step Checklist
- ☐ Create your Staying Centered card.
- ☐ Apply the Staying Centered principles and record your reflections.

Have you ever built a snowman? You start with that little ball of packed snow and roll it around…and then all of a sudden it starts growing…and growing…and growing…faster and faster. This is what happens in our minds when we aren't aware and/or present in the moment. What starts out as a little doubt or anxiety can roll into sadness and then depression. What starts out as a little frustration can roll into resentment and then anger.

Most of us have multiple thoughts in our minds. When we focus on the external, they quickly gain momentum. When we aren't living in the moment, we rarely have positive thoughts that spiral with the same momentum as the negative. Instead, our positive experiences become a little sun that melts a bit of snow, but then the automatic negative thought process begins again, building and building and building. Often the "source" of the snowball is one little external event—it doesn't take much to start the process.

Let Me Give a Couple Examples

A couple has been working very hard to stash away money for a family vacation. Over the past few years, due to an unexpected illness not covered by insurance, they have gone into great debt. They were initially very frustrated at the unfairness of it all but vowed to retake control over their finances. Many heated discussions ensued (as often do with finances), but they finally are on the mend and saving money for a family vacation.

This particular morning, their water heater went out. They called the service team, and it turns out it will need to be replaced. The cost is $800. So far, they have $500 in their vacation savings, and that has taken four months to accumulate. The wife points out that they don't have enough saved for this unexpected event. The husband points out that they would need to save for two and a half more months just to afford the repair, then another eight months to resave for the vacation. The vacation that they had been working so hard toward, that had been in the foreseeable future, now seems twelve months away—if they're lucky. Unable to think of another option, they use a credit card—which they had vowed not to use as part of their debt-reduction plan—to pay for the new water heater. Later that night, the husband wonders why they bother trying to save anyway, since things never go their way. The wife shares with the children that the vacation they had hoped to take shortly was now out of the picture for a while. The teenage daughter gets very upset, wondering why her parents make promises they cannot keep. The wife goes to bed in tears, thinking she is a bad mother. She also feels guilt that her home isn't happier and that she has failed as a wife and mother. The husband lies awake feeling guilty that he can't be a good provider like his father was.

Here's Another Example

Josephine has been trying to regain control of her life, which seems to have spiraled out of control. Josephine is a wife and a stay-at-home mother of three children under ten. Lately she has been feeling unfulfilled and that she has little room to think or pursue her passions—even though she can't quite recall what her passions were prior to becoming a wife and mother.

It is winter outside, the snow is falling, and going anywhere requires extra time to dress the kids, extra time to drive—everything requires extra time, which is the one thing Josephine has a shortage of to begin with.

On this particular day, Josephine has gotten up early, as the kids had an overnight with their grandmother last night. She has made a plan to clean the house top to bottom and then maintain it on a weekly basis. She has also decided to redo her diet, thinking better nutrition might help with the funk she has been in lately. Last week she signed up for the local gym and plans on trying out her membership tonight.

This morning, however, she isn't feeling as good as she had hoped and woke up a bit late. She is sniffling, perhaps coming down with her youngest child's latest cold. She passes the mirror and notices the bags under her eyes. A quick glance at her reflection makes her glad she joined the gym. She shakes herself out of it and gets to work.

Soon she is in the groove, bagging piles to take to charity and garbage to haul out. Her three children arrive home that evening.

No one seems to notice all the cleaning she has done; instead they want to know what's for dinner. Josephine's husband arrives home a short while later and doesn't remove his boots, leaving marks all over the clean floor. He then puts a pile of mail on her clean countertop. A short three hours later, the work she did seems invisible beneath the "activity" of the evening, and no one has praised her. She wonders why she bothered to clean in the first place. Originally she was going to go to the gym tonight, but now she is not in the mood. Instead, she feels like crawling back into bed—but there are babies to be washed, and she has to get everything together for church the following day.

Later that night as she lies awake in bed, she wonders, *What's it all for? Why can't I just enjoy my home and family? What's wrong with me?*

Although these stories may seem melodramatic, they are pretty representative of how we perceive certain events to be in our minds. Problems often appear bigger than they are. And the bigger they appear, the quicker they snowball.

Keeping in mind the earlier illustration, reread each story, and see if you can identify what is happening and how the "core" of each issue is based on the external—thus fluctuating with the external circumstances.

Example One

The "external event" at the core for this couple is money. Their contentment doesn't lie within themselves; instead it varies with their level of debt. When they feel they are making progress, things are hunky-dory. When things go awry, the spiral begins.

Core Centeredness depends on:
- Money
- Family vacation

Snowball:
- Unexpected house maintenance (external)
- Realization of setback and debt (external)
- Using a credit card they didn't want to use (external)

These events then pile up and create circle two—how they perceive themselves:
- Sense of hopelessness (internal)
- Sense of being a "poor" spouse or parent (internal)

In a matter of twenty-four hours, this couple went from being on the path to a family vacation to feeling guilty about their relationship and parenting abilities. Quite a snowball. William Shakespeare said, "Nothing is either good or bad but thinking makes it so." Let's unravel the thought path that led to the couples' conclusions.

The first question in fact finding is to ask, **what exactly happened here?** This is not a subjective question open to interpretation but a fact-finding mission. In this case, the answer would be that a water heater broke. Taking stock of what actually happened is the first step in stopping the snowball. The next question to ask is, **what does this mean?** In this example, it would mean that the family no longer has hot water. There you have it: the situation in a nutshell. If you look at it objectively, that is what you see.

Now, let's look at what the couple did by linking their "centeredness" to an external circumstance like money. Because this was at their core, they couldn't be objective: *they were too emotionally close to the situation*. Since they didn't have a centered place from which to gather strength, they did not have clear boundaries. They felt having money was essential to having less stress and thus a stronger relationship. They also felt that being able to provide a vacation was important to be good parents. In their minds, the water heater didn't break—their family broke, because their thinking had knotted everything together.

You might be wondering, what else could they have done? They had no hot water and no backup resources. That brings us to the third question to ask: **what choices do I have here?** In this instance, the family did not stop to evaluate and brainstorm. Instead, their thinking went on autopilot and quickly ended in a snarl of guilt. If they had a strong and centered core, they would have been able to stop and ask some helpful questions such as:

How important is this vacation? What does it mean to us? What are ways we can still accomplish both? Is there another vacation we might take? And finally, they could come up with a centered answer for the last staying-centered question: **what choice feeds my soul and makes me feel good?**

A broken water heater is not the end of the world, and it certainly is not a reflection of parenting skills. Yet when we don't think clearly, we can quickly make distorted connections like the one in this example. Had I been with this couple during this event, I would have commended them on the strides they had taken to get out of debt. I would have realized quickly that their self-worth was somehow tied into this vacation, which was why they were having such a strong reaction. While there would be no way to teach them all the principles on the spot—they would have to know them prior to coming into a situation like this—I would encourage them to *untie the knot* through a reality check based on the following questions:

- What is the worst thing that can happen here?
- What is the best thing that can happen here?
- What is something in between that can happen here?

From their perspective, the worst thing would be that they would return to a debt-filled life and the stress they had worked so hard to escape. Yet if we talked that through, we would quickly realize that this is an overreaction. Their past debt was created because they continually overspent. This is a different situation. Using a charge card in this emergency doesn't mean they are returning to a debt-filled lifestyle.

On the flipside, the best thing would be that $1,000 would fall from the sky or the water heater would start working again.

The balanced and centered decision doesn't rely on highs or lows, so we would then pursue the last question: what is something in-between that can happen here? I would encourage them to put the water heater on their credit card and still go on their vacation, being careful not to overspend. Or to pay $200 toward the water heater in cash and charge the $600, with a clear plan for paying it off in the next eight months, instead of sacrificing their vacation. They could then use the remaining cash to take a vacation that was a little less expensive.

Example Two
Can you guess what Josephine's core is tied to? The external event affecting Josephine is "having everything in order" along with "approval and praise from family." Josephine is not actively creating esteem within; therefore she seeks esteem from those around her through praise and approval. This "approval addiction" and need to please is very common among women.

Core Centeredness depends on:
- Organization
- Approval

Snowball:
- Not feeling well physically (external)
- Waking up late (external)
- Family demands for dinner (external)
- Husband not noticing work, dirtying clean floor (external)
- House looking messy after three hours (external)
- No recognition (external)

These events then pile up and create circle two—how Josephine perceives herself:
- No longer wants to go to the gym (internal)
- Wonders what is wrong with her (internal)

Let's see how the fact finding might have helped Josephine recover. Had she used this practice while facing the situation (which is what I encourage you to do this week), she would have asked, **what is actually happening here?** The answer would be that her house is dirtier than she would like. **What does that mean?** The answer would be, simply, that her house is dirtier than she would like. If we don't stop and "audit" our thoughts we go down a path like this: *My dirty house means I have poor time management. I can't take care of my family as well as other people can. I am never able to make a system work.* Can you see how quickly a snowball can form?

Being aware of and auditing our thoughts as they occur will stop the spiraling snowball. If Josephine had done this, she could then ask, **what are my choices?** She had many, although she wouldn't see them until she stopped and took stock. This is very important, as we tend to become sad, anxious, or depressed when we feel we do not have any options.

Here are some choices I can think of for Josephine:

- Have a family meeting and explain the stress of the household. Ask for help in maintaining the clean home.
- Develop a chore and reward system.
- Have a friend over and clean together; then clean her house the following week.
- Hire a cleaning service.
- Make cleaning fun with a class like Extreme Home Makeover and "cleaning sprints."
- Decide on a personal reward system instead of relying on external praise.

I am sure you can add a few ideas to this list. Josephine could then ask the last question, **what feeds my soul and makes me feel good?** The answer to this question should be internal, not external. We aren't concerned with what feeds everyone else's soul—just our own. What do we need to stay centered and balanced? Becoming centered, peaceful, and balanced is the best thing we can do to nourish those around us.

Staying Centered

What exactly happened here?
What does this mean?
Where are my choices?
    If you get stuck on this question, brainstorm with…
        What is the worst that could happen?
        What is the best that could happen?
        What is something in between that could happen?
What would feed my soul and make me feel good?

Observe what is at your center. Note your moods a couple of times each day, especially when you find yourself happy or down. Ask, **what is behind this?** Determine whether it is external or internal. An internal example would be that you are creating this feeling. We can create moments of happiness by living in the moment, enjoying a process, being compassionate. We can create unhappy moments by dwelling on the past, worrying, doubting, and belittling ourselves and others. An external example means it is tied to another person or an external situation.

When you find yourself sad, anxious, worried, angry, or depressed, sit down and write out your answers to these questions in your journal.

mini-makeover

recapturing daily magic
part one: back to basics

"The Constitution only guarantees the American people the right to pursue happiness. You have to catch it yourself."—*Benjamin Franklin*

Why is happiness so elusive, here one moment and gone the next? How do we recapture magic and happiness in our lives? I set out to answer that question in 2007 and created a Happiness Toolbox I could turn to whenever I felt the need to give my life a happiness tune-up. In Recapturing Daily Magic Parts One and Two, I share two key areas that influence happiness: getting back to basics and then connecting with others beyond ourselves.

Action Step Checklist
- [ ] Complete the Today Instead of Tomorrow reflection question.
- [ ] Complete the Monday through Sunday list.
- [ ] Answer the No Comparisons reflection questions.
- [ ] Complete the Giving up the Rat Race reflections exercise.
- [ ] Complete the Signature Strengths reflection question.
- [ ] Complete the Becoming Mindful of the Moment activity.
- [ ] Continue the Riches reflection exercise for thirty days.

In the 1900s scientific journals published about a hundred studies on sadness for every one study on happiness. Fortunately a shift has occurred and researchers are now asking, what makes people happy? Interestingly, research is conclusive that people aren't very good at predicting what will make them happy; when asked, common answers include luxury, money, influence, and beauty — none of which match the new findings of what actually brings us happiness.

In a *USA Today* article, Harvard University psychologist Daniel Gilbert commented, "There's a reason why Euripides said, 'It would not be better if men got what they wanted.'" People expect that events will have a larger and more enduring impact on them — for good or ill — than they really do, Gilbert's studies find.

So what does make people happy?

Tip: As you work through the Recapturing Daily Magic Minis, record your reflections on each of the activities. These reflections will help you know which steps are most influential for your own Happiness Toolbox.

Schedule Living for Today Instead of Tomorrow

Research shows that we need to have more fun today instead of thinking about having fun tomorrow. Just like we put off relationships, we may put off what we truly want and desire to do until after our must-do list is complete. Must-do lists are never complete — at least not while we are living! Take time every day, even if it is just a little bit of time, to do something you want to do. Tomorrows are not promises, just hopes. Today is our only guarantee. Let's live it while we have it.

Reflections:
Where have you sacrificed your want-to-dos for your must-dos to the point that you never arrive at your want-to-dos?

List ten things you find yourself saying you want to do, if only you could find the time:

_____

_____

_____

_____

_____

_____

_____

_____

Sometimes items on our want-to-do list seem to be too big to fit neatly into a day. Yet instead of waiting for the "right time," I encourage you to break these items down. For example, I found myself saying "I want to catch up on my photo albums" time and time again, yet I was unable to find the time to do so. I broke that project down by taking one set of photos and choosing the paper, backgrounds, stickers, scissors, embellishments, etc., for the pages during a couple of twenty-minute "me times." Then I placed each two-page spread in a twelve-by-twelve envelope (making sure to include a glue stick and scissors). The project that seemed tied to my craft supplies was now completely portable; it could even accompany me in the car. By doing this, I could enjoy working on the pages even if I only had ten or fifteen minutes to do so.

How can you incorporate some of your want-to-dos daily? For each day listed, write in one simple activity you can do that is not a need-to-do but a want-to-do.

Monday

_____

_____

Tuesday

_____

_____

Wednesday

_____

_____

Thursday

_____

_____

Friday

_____

_____

Saturday

_____

_____

Sunday

_____

_____

No Comparisons

I had an interesting conversation with a girlfriend the other day. She was telling me about this woman who "has it all." My friend perceives this woman as having the most perfect and caring husband; beautiful, talented, and respectful children; and a well-kept and beautiful home — and the woman herself is beautiful with a great attitude. The description concluded with an exclamation like, "I just hate her!" (said tongue in cheek).

I started laughing. My friend asked me what was so funny. I posed this question, "If this woman had an awful husband, ugly children, a shack, and a bad attitude, would that make *your* life better?"

She asked me what that had to do with anything. I proceeded to ask her why she was spending so much time analyzing this woman's life, what possible purpose did it serve? She explained that if this woman could "have it all," then certainly she could as well. "But what if this woman didn't have it all?" I pressed on. "Would that mean you couldn't have it all?"

Whether this woman owned a llama farm or was an attorney, First Lady, or the first female President of the United States has no bearing on my friend's life. Each moment she spent looking at this woman and comparing lives was taking her focus off of where it needed to be: her own life. Whatever this woman's life looks like is completely irrelevant to all of us. It doesn't change our life one iota. The only thing that can change our lives is us. Mother Teresa once said, "Your life is what you make it" — not what others make it.

We rarely compare ourselves to those who have less to increase our self-esteem, but women often compare themselves to those who have more, thereby undermining their self-esteem. Embrace the concept of looking at your own life instead of the lives of others. Don't be distracted with the destructive thinking that comes from comparing yourself to another person — especially since you can never truly walk in his or her shoes.

Reflections:

Who do you compare yourself to?

_____

_____

_____

How do these comparisons hinder or help you?

_____

_____

_____

How would it feel to let go of measuring your life against the lives of others?

_____

_____

_____

Make a copy of the following affirmation and tape it to a business card to keep in your wallet. Each time you compare yourself to someone else, slowly read the card (either aloud or in your head) several times.

Today, I only compare myself to the "me" I was yesterday.

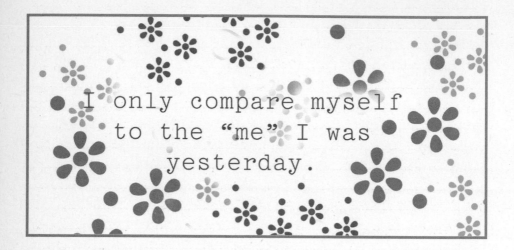

I only compare myself to the "me" I was yesterday.

Giving Up the Rat Race

"The problem with the rat race is even if you win, you're still a rat."
—*Lily Tomlin*

"Materialism is toxic for happiness," says University of Illinois psychologist Ed Diener. Even rich materialists aren't as happy as those who care less about getting and spending.

Sarah Bernhardt said, "It is by 'spending' oneself that one becomes rich." I cannot imagine truer words. "Being rich" is not a matter of having money. It's a matter of experiencing life, enjoying the moment, involving yourself with your children, family, and friends; it's committing to a cause of great importance to you, learning new ideas, keeping an involved and educated mind, feeling with all your heart—those are the riches that are measured by a full life, not the ones you "take to the bank."

Reflections:
What riches exist in your life? Challenge yourself to list fifty riches over the course of the next thirty days.

Signature Strengths

One of my mentors is a very successful CEO who has gone through vigorous, top-notch, elite training programs. When I asked him for advice, he shared that the single most important thing people can do is recognize their core competencies. He explained that there are things in this world that <u>only</u> I can do. He stressed that I needed to spend 90 percent of my time "in that zone." He also explained that there are many things I can do that others can do also. He shared that one of the biggest mistakes we make is not being true to our core competencies and spending too much time doing things that other people can also do.

Our core competencies, or signature strengths, are often things we love doing—we get lost in them. "Flow" is the term author and psychologist Mihaly Csikszentmihaly uses to describe this sensation: "People in flow may be sewing up a storm, doing brain surgery, playing a musical instrument, or working a hard puzzle with their child. The impact is the same: A life of many activities in flow is likely to be a life of great satisfaction."

Sometimes we do this because we think "our way is the best way" or because we are scared to let go. But each time we veer from our signature strengths, we also veer from our core mission.

Reflections:
What are your signature strengths? What tasks do you need to let go of so you can spend more time "in that zone"?

_____

_____

_____

_____

_____

Staying in the Moment

Think of three times in your life when you were truly happy. They don't have to be the happiest times of your life, just times when you were undeniably happy. Once you have visualized these moments, consider the following: During these happy moments were you...

- worried about finances?
- preoccupied with a potentially stressful event that was coming
- up the following week?
- worried about whether your boss would like the work you turned in?
- contemplating the ten thousand loads of laundry that needed to be done?

Even if you were experiencing financial stress, job worry, or laundry woes in your life, you likely answered no to all of the above. One similarity that you will find in 99 percent of these moments is that when you feel truly happy, you are living in the moment. While something external might have influenced the happiness, your mind also made the decision to filter out the past and future, to live in the now.

Happiness involves absorption in the moment. Woes and worries fade to the background as the mind filters out the past and preoccupation with the future to experience the now.

Why is living in the moment tied to happiness? Because right at this very moment, this very second when you are reading these words, life isn't so bad, is it? I mean, you have a computer; you are able to read; you are taking positive steps; you must be somewhere safe and private if you are reading this. Right this second, everything is okay. Yet when you make the decision to overlook that and pull in all your worries of tomorrow and regrets of yesterday, you detach from the moment. Guess what happens to your mood then? It goes up or down in correlation to what you are thinking about.

I can worry about tomorrow for hours today—it doesn't do me any good. Worry is a negative emotion, and it drains us. We worry when something is out of our control. If something is out of our control, why waste the present moment trying to control it? Since it is out of our control, focusing on the task creates more worry. What actually happens in the moments of the future cannot be determined right now, in this moment.

I can spend hours of my day feeling guilty about a decision I made years ago, a week ago, a day ago or an hour ago. My guilt does not change what happened in the past. Like worry, guilt is a negative and draining emotion. Like it or not, I can't do magic, I can't change the past. But I can change this moment.

I can spend hours of my day blaming others for my current predicament. Each moment I focus on blame, I give up my power to create a positive reality.

When we learn to stay in the moment, we make decisions that reduce worry by creating a solid foundation for the days to come, while also living each day more fully, which, in turn, reduces guilt about the past.

Happiness is created when thoughts fully absorb the present. If thoughts turn to regrets of yesterday, we become regretful. If thoughts turn to anxieties of tomorrow, we become anxious. If we try to be present in the moment but our mind wanders back and forth, our mood goes up and down in correlation. The now is lost when mixed with yesterday's regrets and tomorrow's worries. While living in the moment seems conceptually simple, we are accustomed to living in a preoccupied state.

When we lose focus on this very moment, we also become incapable of creating change; I can't accomplish anything tomorrow by thinking about it today. All I have is today, this moment. I can't change anything I did yesterday by thinking about it. I can take something I learned yesterday and implement it today, but I can't change the past. I can anticipate tomorrow and prepare for it today, but I can't change tomorrow, because it doesn't exist yet. All I can work with is the moment at hand. Stress and worry about yesterday will only lead to further regret. Regret is a compilation of moments we have missed. If we don't live in the moment today, we are going to add to the regrets we feel tomorrow. When we spend too much energy focusing on yesterday or worrying about tomorrow, we drain the attitude and action we have available in the present moment.

Activity: Becoming Mindful of the Moment
Living in the moment seems conceptually simple, but it is difficult to make it a habit, because we are so accustomed to living in a preoccupied or distracted state. The best exercise I have found for increasing mindfulness is to choose one activity you do frequently throughout the day, such as washing your hands, looking in the mirror, getting something to drink, opening your front door, closing your car door, etc., and using this action as a "prompt." Just choose one activity. Then each time you do that activity, use it as a mental prompt to bring your focus "back to the moment." By practicing this technique again and again, you will soon find yourself mastering the concept of mindfulness. Work with one mental prompt this week; then next week add another.

How will you become more mindful? What prompt will you try? Make some notes on how this awareness influences daily magic.

mini-makeover

recapturing daily magic
part two: beyond ourselves

"Let no one ever come to you without coming away better and happier."
—*Mother Teresa*

Research suggests that altruistic acts boost happiness in the giver; making someone else's day can dramatically help make your day better. This simple practice doesn't take any additional time; it only requires your awareness of others. At every opportunity you find today, pay someone a sincere compliment or do something nice for another person. Hold the door for the people behind you. When you park your car at the grocery store, offer to take the cart back in for someone who is just unloading his or her groceries. These simple acts of kindness change the lives of others while also changing our own.

Action Step Checklist
- ☐ Make a Kindness Card to use throughout the week.
- ☐ Complete the Forgiveness reflection questions.
- ☐ Answer the Releasing Blame and Expectations reflection questions.
- ☐ Complete the Put People at the Center reflection questions.
- ☐ Complete the Go with the Flow reflection questions.

Giving Back

In my own life, I can recall simple acts of kindness that were extended toward me, leaving a smile on my face throughout the day. Two years ago I was walking through an airport in Toronto and a businesswoman on a cell phone stopped in the middle of her conversation and quickly said "nice boots" before turning back to her phone call and continuing on to her destination. Two simple words that left a smile on my face and that I still remember vividly. Little did she know I had purchased the boots and then had hemmed and hawed over the purchase because they were more than I was used to spending. Of course this woman may never remember that moment, but she put a smile on my face that day.

I also remember a day when I was in a grocery store checkout line. I can't remember what tabloid I had picked up, but I was laughing with the cashier about a story while she scanned my groceries. Placing her groceries on the belt behind me was an elderly woman.

The cashier and I continued to banter, both of us laughing wholeheartedly. Then the elderly woman added a one-liner that made us laugh even harder. I gently gave the elderly woman a squeeze while I continued laughing. The elderly woman looked at me, startled, and said, "That was the first hug I've had all week. Thank you." I then gave her another one. Of course, I could have just gone through the checkout lane without ever talking to anyone, reading the silly tabloid to myself or focusing on the next errand on my to-do list.

Tomorrow, smile and offer random acts of kindness when you can. Stop by the message board to let us know how this influenced your day.

Activity: Making a Kindness Card
Copy the following Kindness Card and paste it onto a three-by-five card. Then tuck it into your planner. Each week challenge yourself to fill it with kindnesses you do for others.

Forgiveness

"Letting go is an act of strength and courage. It helps healing begin, frees you of the weight of the past, and opens doors to a new future."—*Stephanie Tourles*, Lift Me Up

According to University of Michigan psychologist Christopher Peterson, forgiveness is the trait most strongly linked to happiness. "It's the queen of all virtues and probably the hardest to come by," he says.

We cannot be our best when we are holding on to grudges. An unforgiving mind or heart is like a heavy anchor, and whether we feel it or not, it will pull us down.

One of the areas I have worked in extensively is grief and bereavement. When I was speaking at a conference for bereaved parents in South Carolina, I met a man who changed my view of forgiveness forever. He had lost two children in a car accident. The driver of the other vehicle was intoxicated. These were his only two daughters, and they were on their way to a rehearsal dinner for the oldest daughter's wedding. As we talked, he told me he had forgiven the driver, although it had taken several years. I tried to put myself in his shoes—would I be able to forgive? I would like to think I could, but at that time, I was not so sure.

I asked him how he had forgiven him—and I also asked him why. He looked me straight in the eye and said, "I had no choice. To hold on to my anger would have tied me to him forever. To hold on to my anger would have killed me, too."

This man knew at the depth of his soul that his anger could never help him, but it could destroy or distract him from finding any joy for the rest of his days. "My daughters would not want that," he stated firmly.

Is there anyone you might consider forgiving? Even if you are not ready to do so, take a moment to write down whom.

Reflections:
How does being unforgiving help or hurt you?

_____
_____
_____
_____
_____

Is anger weighing you down in life?

_____
_____
_____
_____

What negative emotional clutter can you clear to increase the space available for joy?

_____
_____
_____
_____

Consider writing about an experience you need to forgive in detail. Then rip the paper into tiny shreds as a way to release and symbolically let go.

Releasing Blame and Expectations

"Expect nothing. Live frugally on surprise."—*Alice Walker*

When a friend of mine was going through some challenging times, I asked her what solutions she could brainstorm. Each of her solutions relied on someone else: "If only she could..." "If they would just..." "He should have..."

Sometimes the expectations we have of others can interfere with our ability to live a rich and rewarding life. Studies show that autonomy and the ability to have a sense of control and choice in regard to our surroundings is a key component of happiness. When expectations prevent taking action and responsibility, we limit personal power and build a roadblock on the path to happiness.

In a study published in the February 2008 issue of the Journal of Personality and Social Psychology, psychologists revealed the findings of a new happiness research. It turns out money, luxury, and influence are not at the top of influencing factors. Topping the list of needs that appear to bring happiness are autonomy (feeling that your activities are self-chosen and self-endorsed), competence (feeling that you are effective in your activities), relatedness (feeling a sense of closeness with others), and self-esteem.

These findings are important, say the study authors, because, once identified, "psychological needs can be targeted to enhance personal thriving, in the same way that the organic needs of plants, once identified, can be targeted to maximize thriving in the plant."

We cannot control other people, regardless of how well we know them or how close we are. Anytime we do try to control another person, we are engaging in unhealthy patterns and manipulation. We are not qualified to control other people; we have a hard enough time controlling our own thoughts and actions. The journey of life calls on us to learn to control our own thoughts and actions.

To "expect nothing" as Alice Walker encourages, is not about giving up hope but releasing expectations. Instead of placing our needs in the hands of others, we place them where they belong: in our own hands and in our own faith.

When we put our needs in our own hands, then the positive actions of others become blessings versus expectations. We don't feel let down if something doesn't happen but inspired when something does.

Reflections:
What needs have you given others to fulfill for you? What have the results been?

_____

_____

_____

_____

_____

Whom are you waiting on in order to move forward, and what are you waiting on specifically?

_____

_____

_____

What step can you take today to recall at least one of these needs and put it back in the only place it can be fulfilled: in your own hands?

_____

_____

_____

Put People at the Center

University of Pennsylvania psychologist Martin E. P. Seligman, author of the book *Authentic Happiness*, discovered the happiest people spend the least time alone.

We are all susceptible to the paradox of living our lives backward. We put our to-dos at the center of our life and put spending time with those we love <u>after</u> we meet our to-dos. Often that can mean that our time with others is cut short. While certain times and seasons will require more to-dos than others, science has shown that enriching human interaction is at the center of the happiness equation, ranking above money, status, and health. We must maintain our connection to the people we love. You will find an activity for checking the strength of your connections on the following pages.

Here are some simple ways to connect with others and show them you care:

- Look into their eyes when you talk to them
- Listen with undivided attention
- Set boundaries that keep relationships healthy
- Be honest
- Ask for their opinion
- Be yourself
- Listen to their stories and share your own
- Say you are sorry when you are wrong
- Forget your worries and keep the focus on the other person
- Validate their feelings
- Ask questions
- Give space when needed
- Tell others you value them
- Show others you value them through a card, call, or note
- Be consistent

Reflections:
Which people are at the core of your life? Family? Friends? List them out by name on the worksheet. As you look at your week, are you spending enough time with the people that matter most to you? Avoid letting your to-dos take away from spending time with the people that make life worth living and to-dos worth doing.

The people who are most important in my life right now are...

_____

_____

_____

In the next seven days, I currently have the following events confirmed to spend time with these people.

Event and Hours Planned

_____

_____

_____

_____

_____

_____

_____

_____

_____

_____

_____

_____

_____

How many hours of events do you have scheduled with others?

_____

If you find the answer is low, list out action steps you will take within the next seventy-two hours to change it. (Writing the list alone won't help! Make sure check it off by following through.)

_____

_____

_____

_____

_____

_____

_____

_____

Go with the Flow

Every year in the small town where my mother, brother, and I grew up, a barefoot water-ski tournament is held in my brother's memory (Caleb was a renowned and recognized skier).

This heavily wooded little town holds about six hundred people year round and thousands in the summer. Its main attraction is a chain of nine lakes connected by channels. If you have a boat or love the water, this is the place to be.

Life moves at a slower pace there—or maybe life goes at the pace it should, and we just move faster elsewhere. There aren't any drive-through fast-food options for over twenty-five miles, so you actually have to plan what you are going to do for meals. Stores still close at 4:00 and 5:00 p.m., so commitments don't eat into the night-time hours. There isn't a gym or fitness center for miles, so you'll see many people swimming in the lake, walking, jogging, or biking. Hotels don't have high-speed Internet access, and there isn't a Best Buy to grab a new computer game to keep a young one busy.

Going up north reminds me to go with the flow. My friend Sara was with me on last year's visit, and our hotel did not have a hair-dryer, shampoo, or Internet. We arrived with forty-eight hours to help complete a long list of duties for the ski tournament. Our cell phones were out of range in many places; and every task required at least forty miles of driving round-trip.

We realized we had a choice: we could go with the flow or become stressed because of everything we needed to do that couldn't get done due to the "inefficiencies" of missing items and the driving distances required. After I washed my hair with only an eighth of an inch of hotel soap, I connected with Sara for the daily duties. We both had the same attitude about going with the flow and letting the days unfold versus trying to create a "certain day." For both of us, this made a big difference in our ability to enjoy and cherish the many moments that were to come.

Reflections:
How often do you get stressed versus going with the flow?

_____

_____

_____

_____

_____

Where in your life do you focus on things outside of your control?

_____

_____

_____

_____

How often do you try to create a certain memory or day versus letting the day unfold and bring its gifts to you?

_____

_____

_____

_____

_____

> ***Try It:*** *Start your day with a good intention and solid plan of action, but when things go awry or off plan, don't miss the gifts the day might have in store because you are so busy trying to push the day back into something that it just isn't.*

mini-makeover

facing fear and stepping outside the comfort zone

"Nobody ever died of discomfort, yet living in the name of comfort has killed more ideas, more opportunities, more actions, and more growth than everything else combined."—*T. Harv Eker*

While there are many types of fear, the fear we explore in this Mini is "good fear." Good fear often causes a bit of discomfort, anxiety, and nervousness but serves as a healthy calling to step past our existing comfort zones into uncharted territory. Ignored or unaddressed for a period of time, good fear and its healthy callings often turn into lost opportunities, regrets, severe anxiety, or complacency.

Action Step Checklist
- ☐ Read and answer Reflection Question #1.
- ☐ Read and answer Reflection Question #2.
- ☐ Create the List in Reflection Question #3.
- ☐ Read Luke's story.
- ☐ Read and answer Reflection Question #4.
- ☐ Read and answer Reflection Question #5.
- ☐ Read and answer Reflection Question #6.
- ☐ Read and answer Reflection Question #7.
- ☐ Complete the Reality Check worksheet.
- ☐ Complete the Stepping Forward worksheet.
- ☐ Create the Pocket Tool.

"Death is not the biggest fear we have; our biggest fear is taking the risk to be alive—the risk to be alive and express what we really are."
—*Don Miguel*

At the outset, fear seems to be an uncomfortable emotion, yet perspective and how we work with fear can turn this seemingly negative emotion into a positive springboard for reaching goals and self-growth.

In areas of goals and self-growth, I have worked with many women who have a strong desire to make changes in their lives. Change requires redefining our current comfort zone. Many people love the idea of having a new comfort zone, yet when the call to step outside the comfort zone comes, they make a decision that allows them to avoid fear and discomfort. These people opt not to walk the tightrope, cross the line, take the chance, or brave the risk, because something scares them. Sometimes it is external, often it is the monsters people make in their own minds.

Reflection Question #1: What does the word "fear" mean to you? When you think of the word, what images come to mind?

_____

_____

_____

_____

Reflection Question #2: How would your relationship with fear change if you thought of it as a calling for change or potential growth?

_____

_____

_____

_____

"Fear grows in darkness; if you think there's a boogeyman around, turn on the light."—*Dorothy Thompson*

I want to share the true story that inspired me to write about fear and its ability to control our lives when we don't, as Thompson says, "turn on the light."

Luke's Story

(This story was used with permission, although the name and some identifying information has been changed for privacy.)

Luke is a dear friend of many years. The driving fear in Luke's life stems from his childhood. Luke was born outside of the United States, and his parents struggled to provide for the family. Luke's father died when he was relatively young. In his early twenties Luke became a U.S. citizen and attended a good college on scholarships. He is a brilliant man and hard worker who quickly rose to the top of his field. As a top executive within a large company, he can easily support his family (he is married and has children) while also supporting his birth family in his native country.

Luke and I had been talking for many months about a choice he was struggling with—a big decision coming up in a few months that would affect his family and career. During our many discussions, I had served as a sounding board, guiding him to explore what was truly best for him (and thus those around him) without offering my personal opinion.

One afternoon, Luke called to tell me he had finally decided what he would do when the decision time came in the next several months. After he shared his realization I said that I supported his decision fully and felt he was making the best choice. In the months that followed, we had many discussions in which he again affirmed the action he had chosen.

The night before "decision day," he called. His voice was filled with conviction and purpose; all that remained was "dotting his i's and crossing his t's." Yet I knew that the next day—in the moment of decision—he would come face to face with the deep-rooted fear he had held since childhood. This decision would require him to give up the security and comfort he had known and forge into the unknown. Within twenty-four hours he would have to look that fear in the eye and take the final step to move past it.

Guess the ending: Can you guess what happens next? Think through what you have read so far and make your best guess before continuing.

I didn't hear from Luke on decision day. I waited for a few days and then called him. It turned out that in the final moment, when he looked his fear in the eye, he could not step past it but instead stepped backward and let the fear live. Over the phone he began to recite a list of reasons and justifications as to why this alternative decision was really the best choice. Yet he and I both knew these were just excuses; what had actually happened was that his fear had won.

"Comfort zones are most often expanded through discomfort."
—Peter McWilliams

I am not passing judgment on Luke. I do not believe any one person can pass judgment on anyone. Each of us has to fight our own battles, and we can only truly understand the battles when we are in the shoes of the battler.

However, what became abundantly clear to me after watching this struggle play out in Luke's life is how often I have seen people in a similar struggle: seeking truth, finding it—and then letting fear take it away.

Reflection Question #3: Have you made any monsters in your own life by allowing a fear to grow bigger instead of confronting it?

_____

_____

_____

_____

Reflection Question #4: Are there any areas in your life where you have sought truth or come close to a truth that would cause you to take a leap of faith or step outside your comfort zone? How did you respond? How have you let fear interfere with your opportunities for happiness or success?

_____

_____

Reflection Question #5: When in your life have you faced fear and overcome it? What was the result? When have you faced fear and stepped backward? What was the result?

"You gain strength, courage, and confidence by every experience in which you really stop to look fear in the face. You must do the thing which you think you cannot do."—*Eleanor Roosevelt*

Reflection Question #6: Imagine Eleanor was speaking directly to you. What would she be referring to? What is the "the thing which you think you cannot do"?

Luke called less frequently after that day. In the course of six years, we spoke only a handful of times. Now we talk again regularly. When I asked Luke why he didn't call, he replied, "Talking to you reminded me of a time when I made one of the biggest mistakes of my life." While Luke's choice determined the destiny of a once-in-a-lifetime opportunity, he has learned a lot from the process. He has told me that his entire thinking about fear has changed, and many of his actions demonstrate that he has begun putting his childhood fear to rest.

Reflection Question #7: What fear are you ready to put to rest?

Out of Bounds: How to Step Outside of Your Comfort Zone and Grow

When I was in my late teens, I read Susan Jeffers's book *Feel the Fear and Do It Anyway*. The book changed my life, and the title became one of my personal guidelines for living. I knew that to get from point A to point B, I would have to learn to love fear. Fear would have to be my friend, something that would propel me forward and encourage me to challenge myself, instead of something that would leave me cowering in a corner. It wasn't easy to face my fears: I have obsessive-compulsive disorder (OCD) and attention deficit disorder (ADD). (The ADD was not diagnosed until adulthood; the OCD was diagnosed in my late teens.) With active OCD, my list of fears could have filled a notebook the size of the dictionary. I did not let that discourage me. I knew then, as I know now, change begins with one step—and that meant conquering one fear at a time.

I believe that we can only overcome fear when we embrace it. We acknowledge we are scared and terrified, but we look at the situation from all angles, make the best decision we can, and then we take a deep breath and <u>do it anyway</u>. Fear is often a calling that we need to grow and push past old boundaries to discover wonderful new territories.

Reality-Check Worksheet Instructions

Where in your life do you need to (as Susan Jeffers says) "feel the fear and do it anyway"? Choose an area where you believe fear has been holding you back, and summarize it in a sentence at the top of the worksheet in this Mini. Then work through the following worksheet instructions.

Pocket Tool: Have a phrase handy to use when you start to feel fear, such as "I feel the fear and do it anyway" or "I choose to grow." This acknowledges the onset of your fear, raises your awareness, and will bring to mind the findings on your worksheets. Memorize your chosen phrase and recite it each time the fear surfaces. Add it to your Personal Power Deck.

Fear and Reality Are Different
Know that fears and reality are almost always different. Is your fear rational and something to actually be afraid of? Write down any what-ifs that have been supporting your fear in the boxes labeled "challenge." (List one what-if or concern per box.)

The Two-Part Reality Check
A reality check is a very important step in confronting fear. Instead of letting our mind get tangled in what-ifs, we can examine our concerns or worries.

Let's give the challenges we listed a reality check. Look at the first challenge you recorded: do you honestly believe this might happen? In the percent column, indicate the likelihood of the challenge actually happening (just estimate, like 8 percent, 20 percent, etc.).

Since over 90 percent of what we worry about never actually happens, let's focus on the challenges you gave a likelihood percentage of 90 percent or more. (Feel free to come back to the others and complete this step as well.)

In the space beginning "Then I would," write down what would happen if this challenge actually occurred. For example, I worked with one woman who wanted to leave her current stable career to begin her own business. One of Janet's what-ifs/challenges was, "What if I don't make enough money to pay my bills?" In the "Then I would" box, she wrote, "I would get a job again."

Often people find what they write in the "Then I would" box is not as scary as they originally thought. Our minds make fears bigger; putting them on paper helps put them in perspective.

The bottom box begins, "How I would grow." In this box write down how you believe you would grow by overcoming this fear: how would your life change? Janet, the woman longing to pursue her own business, realized she would leave a job that was stressful and have potential for true happiness.

Sleep On It
After completing the worksheet, let it rest for twenty-four hours. (It is very important to sleep on all of this for a night. Science has

shown sleep is imperative for absorbing and processing in innova-
tive ways the information we gather during the day.

After a good night's sleep, review your worksheet. Is this an area
where the benefits of growth encourage facing your fear? (To help
decide, compare how you might grow to the challenge you listed.) If
so, then create a list of simple steps you can take this month to move
forward. For Janet this meant doing a lot of research on businesses,
getting her finances in order, and talking to her husband about her
dream. Remember, your current comfort zone was unfamiliar at
one point. Think "step," not "leap."

Stepping Forward Worksheet
Write down the simple steps you will take on the Stepping Forward
worksheet. Aim for at least five. After you complete each step, write
down a few sentences about how you feel. Overcoming a fear is
often exhilarating; recording your feelings can help inspire you to
keep stepping past your boundaries.

"We cannot become what we want to be by remaining what we are."
—*Max DePree*

Words of Inspiration
"If you remain in your comfort zone, you will not go any further."
—*Catherine Pulsifer*

"Nobody ever died of discomfort, yet living in the name of comfort has
killed more ideas, more opportunities, more actions, and more growth
than everything else combined."—*T. Harv Eker*

Reality Check Worksheet

Challenge:

_____

_____

_____

Likelihood percentage: _____

Then I would:

_____

_____

_____

How I would grow:

_____

_____

_____

Challenge:

_____

_____

_____

Likelihood percentage: _____

Then I would:

_____

_____

_____

How I would grow:

_____

_____

_____

Stepping Forward Worksheet

The step forward I will take is: Date taken:

_____   _____

_____

_____

How I feel afterward:

_____

_____

_____

The step forward I will take is: Date taken:

_____   _____

_____

_____

How I feel afterward:

_____

_____

_____

The step forward I will take is: Date taken:

_____   _____

_____

_____

How I feel afterward:

_____

_____

_____

My Comfort Zone: A Poem

I used to have a comfort zone where I knew I wouldn't fail.
The same four walls and busywork were really more like jail.
I longed so much to do the things I'd never done before,
But stayed inside my comfort zone and paced the same old floor.
I said it didn't matter that I wasn't doing much.
I said I didn't care for things like commission checks and such.
I claimed to be so busy with the things inside the zone,
But deep inside I longed for something special of my own.
I couldn't let my life go by just watching others win.
I held my breath; I stepped outside and let the change begin.
I took a step and with new strength I'd never felt before,
I kissed my comfort zone goodbye and closed and locked the door.
If you're in a comfort zone, afraid to venture out,
Remember that all winners were at one time filled with doubt.
A step or two and words of praise can make your dreams come true.
Reach for your future with a smile; success is there for you!

—Author Unknown

about the author

Sara Pattow

Brook Noel is the author of nineteen books specializing in life management and balance for today's busy woman. Noel is best known for going "beyond the book" by creating a whole experience to interact with and support her readers. She delivers free motivational podcasts, online Q&A chats, message board interaction, in-person free "coffees" when she travels, and free newsletters delivered regularly to tens of thousands of readers. Her greatest passion is the Make Today Matter Life System Online, which is the basis for *The Change Your Life Challenge*. "I feel like everything I have done or experienced in life has culminated in this program and book. The program isn't just about family time, or menu planning, or procrastination, or organizing—it is about every major area of a woman's life."

Noel was recognized in 2003 as one of the Top 40 Business People Under the Age of 40 by *Business Journal*. She was a spokesperson for the Home Business Association and was featured in its top entrepreneur issue. She is an expert for Club Mom and a spokesperson for the Whirlpool Corporation, specializing in the time crunch of busy moms.

Noel has conducted workshops for and/or appeared on/in: *CNN Headline News, ABC World News, FOX Friends, Woman's World, Our*

Children (National PTA Magazine), *Los Angeles Times,* Cedars-Sinai Medical Systems, *Parent's Journal, Booklist, Foreword, Independent Publisher,* University of Washington, UW-Milwaukee, University of Michigan, Single Parents Association, AM Northwest, *Town & Country, New York Post,* "Ask Heloise," Bloomberg Radio—and hundreds of other publication, shows, and stations.

Brook lives in Wisconsin with her husband, their thirteen-year-old daughter, a golden retriever, a black lab who thinks her name is "Kitty," a Puggle named Roxie, and one very large cat named Tom. She invites readers' feedback at **www.brooknoel.com**.